Airness

A PLAY BY
Chelsea Marcantel

Playscripts

Airness (2nd Ed)
Copyright © 2019 Chelsea Marcantel. ALL RIGHTS RESERVED

Copyright Protection. This play (the "Play") is fully protected under the copyright laws of the United States of America and all countries with which the United States has reciprocal copyright relations, whether through bilateral or multilateral treaties or otherwise, and including, but not limited to, all countries covered by the Pan-American Copyright Convention, the Universal Copyright Convention, and the Berne Convention.

Reservation of Rights. All rights to this Play are strictly reserved, including, without limitation, professional and amateur stage performance rights; motion picture, recitation, lecturing, public reading, radio broadcasting, television, video, and sound recording rights; rights to all other forms of mechanical or electronic reproduction now known or yet to be invented, such as CD-ROM, CD-I, DVD, photocopying, and information storage and retrieval systems; and the rights of translation into non-English languages.

Performance Licensing and Royalty Payments. Amateur and stock performance rights to this Play are controlled exclusively by Playscripts, Inc. ("Playscripts"). No amateur or stock production groups or individuals may perform this Play without obtaining advance written permission from Playscripts. Required royalty fees for performing this Play are specified online at the Playscripts website (www.playscripts.com). Such royalty fees may be subject to change without notice. Although this book may have been obtained for a particular licensed performance, such performance rights, if any, are not transferable. Required royalties must be paid every time the Play is performed before any audience, whether or not it is presented for profit and whether or not admission is charged. All licensing requests and inquiries concerning amateur and stock performance rights should be addressed to Playscripts (see contact information on opposite page).

Inquiries concerning all other rights should be addressed to Playscripts, as well; such inquiries will be communicated to the author and the author's agent, as applicable.

Restriction of Alterations. There shall be no deletions, alterations, or changes of any kind made to the Play, including the changing of character gender, the cutting of dialogue, the cutting of music, or the alteration of objectionable language, unless directly authorized by Playscripts. The title of the Play shall not be altered.

Author Credit. Any individual or group receiving permission to produce this Play is required to give credit to the author as the sole and exclusive author of the Play. This obligation applies to the title page of every program distributed in connection with performances of the Play, and in any instance that the title of the Play appears for purposes of advertising, publicizing, or otherwise exploiting the Play and/or a production thereof. The name of the author must appear on a separate line, in which no other name appears, immediately beneath the title and of a font size at least 50% as large as the largest letter used in the title of the Play. No person, firm, or entity may receive credit larger or more prominent than that accorded the author. The name of the author may not be abbreviated or otherwise altered from the form in which it appears in this Play.

Publisher Attribution. All programs, advertisements, and other printed material distributed or published in connection with the amateur or stock production of the Play shall include the following notice:

Produced by special arrangement with Playscripts, Inc.
(www.playscripts.com)

Prohibition of Unauthorized Copying. Any unauthorized copying of this book or excerpts from this book is strictly forbidden by law. Except as otherwise permitted by applicable law, no part of this book may be reproduced, stored in a retrieval system, or transmitted in any form, by any means now known or yet to be invented, including, without limitation, photocopying or scanning, without prior permission from Playscripts.

Statement of Non-affiliation. This Play may include references to brand names and trademarks owned by third parties, and may include references to public figures. Playscripts is not necessarily affiliated with these public figures, or with the owners of such trademarks and brand names. Such references are included solely for parody, political comment, or other permitted purposes.

Permissions for Sound Recordings and Musical Works. This Play may contain directions calling for the performance of a portion, or all, of a musical work not included in the Play's score, or performance of a sound recording of such a musical work. Playscripts has not obtained permissions to perform such works. The producer of this Play is advised to obtain such permissions, if required in the context of the production. The producer is directed to the websites of the U.S. Copyright Office (www.copyright.gov), ASCAP (www.ascap.com), BMI (www.bmi.com), and NMPA (www.nmpa.org) for further information on the need to obtain permissions, and on procedures for obtaining such permissions.

The Rules in Brief

- DO NOT perform this Play without obtaining prior permission from Playscripts, and without paying the required royalty.
- DO NOT photocopy, scan, or otherwise duplicate any part of this book.
- DO NOT alter the text of the Play, change a character's gender, delete any dialogue, cut any music, or alter any objectionable language, unless explicitly authorized by Playscripts.
- DO provide the required credit to the author(s) and the required attribution to Playscripts in all programs and promotional literature associated with any performance of this Play.

Copyright Basics

This Play is protected by United States and international copyright law. These laws ensure that authors are rewarded for creating new and vital dramatic work, and protect them against theft and abuse of their work.

A play is a piece of property, fully owned by the author, just like a house or car. You must obtain permission to use this property, and must pay a royalty fee for the privilege—whether or not you charge an admission fee. Playscripts collects these required payments on behalf of the author.

Anyone who violates an author's copyright is liable as a copyright infringer under United States and international law. Playscripts and the author are entitled to institute legal action for any such infringement, which can subject the infringer to actual damages, statutory damages, and attorneys' fees. A court may impose statutory damages of up to $150,000 for willful copyright infringements. U.S. copyright law also provides for possible criminal sanctions. Visit the website of the U.S. Copyright Office (www.copyright.gov) for more information.

THE BOTTOM LINE: If you break copyright law, you are robbing a playwright and opening yourself to expensive legal action. Follow the rules, and when in doubt, ask us.

> "In music, as in everything, the disappearing moment of experience is the firmest reality."
>
> —Benjamin Boretz

> "You don't choose air guitar. Air guitar chooses you."
>
> —C-Diddy, 2003 World Air Guitar Champion

Cast of Characters

SHREDDY EDDY

GOLDEN THUNDER

FACEBENDER

CANNIBAL QUEEN

THE NINA

D VICIOUS

ANNOUNCER / SPRITE EXEC / HOODED FIGURE

Character Notes

Each character represents one of the pillars of air guitar. This pillar is reflected in performance, song choice, approach to the competition, and personal interactions with others while in character. Mostly, the characters go by their noms d'air. Except for Nina and D Vicious where indicated, they are always wearing the exaggerated costumes of their onstage personas.

All characters are in their 20s or 30s; any part can be played by an actor of any race, except: Golden Thunder, who should be an actor of color, and Facebender, who should be white. Facebender should also be older than the rest of the group by a few years.

Ed "Shreddy Eddy" Leary: artistic merit
Gabe "Golden Thunder" Partridge: originality
Mark "Facebender" Lender: feeling
Astrid "Cannibal Queen" Anderson: technical ability
Nina "The Nina" O'Neal: airness
David "D Vicious" Cooper: charisma/stage presence

Announcer/Sprite Exec/Hooded Figure— These parts are played by the same actor; sometimes his/her voice may be heard, without the actor being onstage. Whenever possible, cast a member of the local air guitar community. You'll be really stoked that you did.

Setting

All scenes take place in dirty, dingy bars in urban areas across the US—some small, some very large—except where indicated in the stage directions.

Each bar has the same setup: a bar with bar stools serving drinks, a stage, and a backstage/green room area with chairs and couches.

A Note on Performance

This play is not meant to mock air guitar or air guitarists. Nothing is being spoofed or sent up in any way. The comedy of the play only works if every character is imbued with sincerity and heart. The personas are big and brash, but they frequently drop to reveal real, earnest, three-dimensional humans with real feelings. Invest in them.

The Scenes

Performances are sixty seconds long, completely choreographed, and astonishingly awesome. They are not half-assed, and they are not jokes. They reveal as much about their performers as the dialogue. Permission to use the following songs is included with your performance license.

Prologue: Last Year's National Championship
- #1: "Cum on Feel the Noize"

Scene 1: Staten Island, New York—Qualifier
- #2: "Sweet Child of Mine"
- #3: "The Supercut of Unity"

Vignette 1: Competition Videos
- #4: "Rebel Yell" (split into Parts 1, 2, and 3)
- #5: "More Than a Feeling"
- #6: "Take It Off"

Scene 2: San Diego, CA—Western Conference Finals
- #7: "Keep on Loving You"

Scene 3: Boston, MA—Mid-Atlantic Conference Finals
- #8: "Arpeggios from Hell"

Vignette 2: D Vicious's Sprite Commercial
- #9: "Crowd Chant"

Scene 4: Chicago, IL—Central Conference Finals
- #10: "I Don't Wanna Grow Up"

Scene 5: New York—Eastern Conference Finals
- #11: "Crowd Chant" clip
- #12: "You Give Love a Bad Name"

Scene 6: New York—After the Loss / Invite to the Dark Horse
- #13: "Sweet Child of Mine" phone clip

Vignette 3: The Dark Horse Competition
- #14: "Shadows of the Night"

Scene 7: Los Angeles—The National Championship
- #15: "Cum on Feel the Noize" slo-mo clip
- #16: "I Love Rock 'N Roll"
- #17: "I Love Rock 'N Roll" instrumental

Official Rules of Competition

(Source: https://www.usairguitar.com/rules)

US Air Guitar obeys the rules set forth by the Air Guitar World Championships:

- Each performance is played to one minute (sixty seconds) of a song.
- The sixty seconds can start anywhere in the song.
- The instrument must be invisible and be a guitar.
- A competitor does not have to live in a city to compete in a qualifier held there.

Rounds

> **Round 1, Freestyle:** Each competitor performs to a song of their choice.
>
> **Round 2, Compulsory:** Top competitors from Round 1 perform surprise song.

Judging Criteria

All performances are scored on a scale from 4.0 to 6.0 — 6.0 being the highest possible. A single score is given to each air guitarist based on their overall performance in that round. The scores from BOTH ROUNDS are added to determine the contestants' final scores. The score reflects the quality of the performance based on three key criteria:

- **Technical merit**
  You don't have to know what notes you're playing, but the more your invisible fretwork corresponds to the music that's playing, the better the performance.

- **Stage presence**
  Anyone can do it in the privacy of their bedroom. Few have what it takes to rock a crowd of hundreds or even thousands—all without an instrument.

- **"Airness"**
  The last criteria is the most difficult to define yet often the most decisive of all. Airness is defined as the extent to which a performance transcends the imitation of a real guitar and becomes an art form in and of itself.

Acknowledgments

Airness premiered at the Humana Festival of New American Plays in March 2017. It was directed by Meredith McDonough with the following cast and staff:

>THE NINA . . . . Marinda Anderson
>ANNOUNCER. . . . . Matt Burns
>CANNIBAL QUEEN. . . . . Angelina Impellizzeri
>SHREDDY EDDY. . . . . Nate Miller
>FACEBENDER . . . . Lucas Papaelias
>GOLDEN THUNDER. . . . . Marc Pierre
>D VICIOUS. . . . . Brian Quijada
>
>Scenic Designer . . . . Deb O
>Costume Designer. . . . . Alison Siple
>Lighting Designer . . . . Paul Toben
>Sound Designer . . . . Lindsay Jones
>Movement Director . . . . Jenny Koons
>Stage Manager . . . . Bekah Wachenfeld
>Dramaturg . . . . Hannah Rae Montgomery
>Casting . . . . Paul Davis, Calleri Casting
>Air Guitar Consultant . . . . Matt "AIRistotle" Burns
>Properties Master . . . . Carrie Mossman
>Production Assistant . . . . Codey Leroy Butler
>Directing Assistant . . . . Lila Rachel Becker
>Assistant Dramaturg . . . . Bryan Howard

Airness owes a developmental debt of gratitude to The Juilliard School.

AIRNESS
by Chelsea Marcantel

Prologue: Last Year's National Championship

[#1: "Cum on Feel the Noize"]

(This scene takes place in memory, so it's outside of time and not set in any particular place. The lights and sound should be impressive, but nowhere near as great as the lights and sound in the final scene. No fog, please! Save that for Scene 7.

We hear the opening notes of an iconic metal banger, Quiet Riot's "Cum on Feel the Noize." As the intro plays, each of our competitors [except Nina] is revealed in his/her own light.

They each have a moment of introduction to the crowd: first SHREDDY EDDY, then GOLDEN THUNDER, then FACEBENDER, then CANNIBAL QUEEN. They strike a pose, like superheroes. IMPORTANT: None of these four characters plays air guitar in this moment.

Finally, D VICIOUS is illuminated. He shreds on air guitar. The others watch him in awe, for about 10 seconds. D VICIOUS is their friend, and he is incredible. As the music ends with a strong finish, the ANNOUNCER raises D VICIOUS's hand over his head.

He's the champion. Elation!)

(BOOM. Blackout.)

Scene 1: Staten Island, New York—Qualifier

(Lights up on a small, dingy bar in Staten Island, New York. It is late afternoon, and there are no patrons here yet, but a few of tonight's competitors have come early to start drinking and get the lay of the land. They are all young, but they are old-timers. They have done this dozens of times before, in a dozen cities and towns.

SHREDDY EDDY, GOLDEN THUNDER, and D VICIOUS sit at the sticky bar, drinking beers. SHREDDY and GOLDEN are in full persona mode. VICIOUS is not playing along.)

D VICIOUS. Worst idea you've ever had, man.

SHREDDY EDDY. Somebody does crucified Jesus every year. Don't be that guy.

GOLDEN THUNDER. "Agent of Unity" is getting me nowhere, dude. I didn't even make the finals in Nashville.

VICIOUS. Nobody gets that you're an "agent of unity." It's like a joke—if you have to explain it, it doesn't work.

GOLDEN. How does it not work? I'm playing an earth-shattering supercut of songs with overt and covert political themes, that tracks the history of "otherized" peoples in America, and ends with the embracement of differences. It's sonic coherence on every level. How are people not putting it together?

SHREDDY. It's a killer supercut, man. But it's maybe just a little bit too much. That's a lot of threads to weave into sixty seconds.

VICIOUS. You don't need to change it, you need to streamline it. Originality only gets you points if the judges can figure out what the hell you're doing.

GOLDEN. But I'm not like you. I start with my message, and then—

VICIOUS. *(interrupting)* It's a rock show, not a lecture, dude.

GOLDEN. The whole impetus of air guitar is world peace, Vicious. If we lose sight of that, *what are we even doing here?*

SHREDDY. I saw a naked guy play his dick in Des Moines this year.

GOLDEN. Aw, come on!

VICIOUS. That happens every year, too, Golden. *(short pause)* Did he place?

SHREDDY. Disqualified for having an instrument onstage.

VICIOUS. Right.

GOLDEN. Is that what this sport is coming to? Surely there are still judges out there with some integrity. I am out here trying to heal the motherfuckin' world, and the world refuses to be healed! *(short pause)* If I don't place here tonight, I'm out. I don't have a hometown qualifier like you, Shreddy, or a free ride to Nationals like his highness over here. If I can't get my message across tonight, I'm out for the season.

VICIOUS. And this will be, what, the fourth year you don't qualify for Nationals?

SHREDDY. Whoa, dude! That's harsh.

VICIOUS. What, is that not a fact? Am I not allowed to bring up the actual fact that neither one of you have ever qualified for the National Championships?

SHREDDY. I mean, you can bring it up. You don't have to be a dick about it. *(short pause)* Last year was your first year at Nationals, and you won the whole thing. One of us could pull that off. Plus, this season, my song is untouchable. Which you would know, if you'd been to *any* of the qualifiers.

VICIOUS. You've always got the perfect song, Shreddy. That's never your problem. Your "angry record store dude" persona's got his head so far up his ass, that you're not giving anything to the crowd. It doesn't matter how superior your taste is, if you can't put on a show.

(A tense pause.)

SHREDDY. Dude, that Sprite commercial really inflated your ego.

GOLDEN. Shit went straight to your head.

VICIOUS. Aw, shut up.

GOLDEN. You aren't even dressed to play the halftime show.

VICIOUS. I've got plenty of time to figure that out.

SHREDDY. What are you playing?

VICIOUS. Got plenty of time to figure that out, too. I'll probably just throw something together in the green room during Round 1.

SHREDDY. *(hurt)* You're not even going to watch us play?

VICIOUS. No offense, my dudes, but I have a lot on my plate right now. I'm only here to play halftime because it's my home turf and I'm doing the organizers a favor. I'm actually thinking of hiring a manager soon. I got lots to get done.

SHREDDY. *(skeptical)* Like what?

> *(FACEBENDER walks into the bar. He pretends to take a guitar case off his back and set it on the stage. He then walks over to SHREDDY, VICIOUS, and GOLDEN.)*

> *(GOLDEN holds out his hand to FACEBENDER, but FACEBENDER bypasses the hand and pulls him into a bear hug.)*

GOLDEN. Facebender! Good to see you, man!

FACEBENDER. Golden Thunder. My dear friend. I hope your journey to New York was pleasant.

GOLDEN. It was all right.

> *(SHREDDY doesn't offer FACEBENDER his hand, but FACEBENDER pulls him into a warm embrace anyway.)*

FACEBENDER. Shreddy Eddy, it fills my heart to the brim to see you hale and hearty.

SHREDDY. Happy to have you in the room, buddy.

FACEBENDER. Happy to be here, friend.

> (FACEBENDER *turns to* VICIOUS *and does an exaggerated, sweeping bow [but he does not hug* VICIOUS*].)*

FACEBENDER. My liege.

VICIOUS. *(enjoying this a little more than he should)* Come on, 'Bender.

> (FACEBENDER *looks around for a bartender, and not seeing one, walks behind the bar, finds a glass, and helps himself.)*

GOLDEN. We haven't seen the bartender in like half an hour.

FACEBENDER. I'll keep track of my own tab. I trust myself.

GOLDEN. *(pause)* Did you catch my song in Nashville, Bender? My supercut of ultimate unity?

FACEBENDER. Indeed I did. I saw the video online.

GOLDEN. What did you think?

FACEBENDER. I thought it was astonishing. Gorgeous, and heartbreaking, and a balm for these troubled times.

GOLDEN. Yeah, see? He gets it. Judges only gave me a 5.1.

FACEBENDER. Egregious!

SHREDDY. The judges at some of these small qualifiers, I mean, who are they? What qualifies them to judge competitive air guitar on our level, you know?

VICIOUS. *(trying to refocus the group's attention on himself)* Most of them wouldn't know a real moment of airness if it smacked them across the face.

GOLDEN. Exactly. And this is the truest art form. The only pure art form left.

FACEBENDER. Incorruptible.

GOLDEN. Un-commercializable.

SHREDDY. Totally democratic.

VICIOUS. And we look fuckin' cool doin' it.

> *(They clink their beer glasses.* VICIOUS *just misses the clink; no one else notices.)*

SHREDDY. But do these new judges understand that? No. They do not. These qualifiers used to be judged by rock gods, real legends.

But now there are so many of them, it's washed-up comedians and satellite radio DJs.

VICIOUS. Not at Nationals.

SHREDDY. No, no, you're right. If we can get to Nationals, we'll be rocking for people who actually appreciate what they're looking at.

FACEBENDER. So let us focus our powers, gentlemen. The hour of triumph is nigh.

> (CANNIBAL QUEEN *enters. She looks around, sees* VICIOUS, *gets a little pissed [he's not where he should be right now] and addresses the guys at the bar.)*

CANNIBAL QUEEN. Hey, Shreddy. Golden. Facebender.

SHREDDY. Hey, CQ.

CANNIBAL QUEEN. *(emphatically)* Cannibal Queen.

FACEBENDER. Care to join us for a pregame libation?

CANNIBAL QUEEN. I'm good. Vicious? I thought we were going to get dinner before the show?

> *(CANNIBAL QUEEN exits.* FACEBENDER, SHREDDY, *and* GOLDEN *make "ooooh, you're in trouble" noises.)*

VICIOUS. *(with great dignity)* Later, Bad News Bears.

> *(VICIOUS exits following* CANNIBAL QUEEN.)

FACEBENDER. She is enchanting.

GOLDEN. That's not the word I'd use.

FACEBENDER. As skilled as she is mysterious. The Aphrodite of air guitar.

SHREDDY. That's excessive, but I will admit, Cannibal Queen's got the best technique in the game right now. There's nothing the judges can pull out in the second round that she can't nail.

FACEBENDER. And yet, she remains as cruelly cast aside as the three of us. Hopes dashed at every qualifier throughout the Midwest, watching her chances of Nationals disappear like ashes in the wind.

GOLDEN. CQ is cold onstage. Low on charisma. She nails it technically, but the crowd comes to have a good time. This isn't Carnegie Hall—

SHREDDY. *(interrupting)* Technical points win championships—

GOLDEN. *(interrupting)* But air guitar's appeal is audience-based. Its whole existence is its effect on the audience, tell me that's not true. Dispute it, if you can, Shreddy. You can't!

SHREDDY. Don't dismiss your technical scores, is all I'm saying. You might be able to fudge your left-hand placement here, in small qualifiers, but on the national stage? The international stage? That just doesn't wash. That's not gonna wash in Finland. Air guitar is not a joke to anyone in Finland.

> *(The air is getting tense.*
> NINA *enters the bar. She looks around. The men stare at her.)*

FACEBENDER. Good evening. Are you lost, miss?

NINA. Not lost. Just early.

FACEBENDER. For the Air Guitar qualifier? I regret to inform you that the show doesn't start for a few more hours.

SHREDDY. I think they open the doors at nine. There's a place with good pizza up the street, if you need to kill time.

NINA. I know what time the show starts. I'm registered to compete.

GOLDEN. Really?

SHREDDY. Fresh meat!

FACEBENDER. Delightful.

SHREDDY. I'm Ed Leary. "Shreddy Eddy."

GOLDEN. Gabe Partridge. "Golden Thunder."

FACEBENDER. And I'm Mark Lender. "Facebender."

NINA. Ed, Gabe, Mark.

GOLDEN. Shreddy Eddy, Golden Thunder, and Facebender.

NINA. Those are your stage names?

SHREDDY. They're our *personas*. Important distinction.

NINA. But you're not onstage.

GOLDEN. We're in the venue, though.

FACEBENDER. We are in the arena. Among its denizens. It has already begun, you see.

NINA. I guess.

SHREDDY. When we're among competitors, we go by our personas.

> *(She stares at them. They stare at her, waiting for her to introduce her persona.)*

NINA. *(after a beat)* I'm Nina.

SHREDDY. What do you go by onstage?

NINA. Are stage names mandatory?

SHREDDY. *Personas.* And they're not. But, like, you gotta have one to protect yourself.

NINA. From what?

SHREDDY. From everything outside the music.

NINA. *(rolling her eyes)* Oh my god.

SHREDDY. When you get up there tonight, you won't be a girl onstage at a dive bar in Staten Island, doing a mime routine. You'll be a rock goddess, playing Wembley Stadium. Madison Square Garden. The International Space Station. Melting faces and breaking hearts for sixty seconds. That rock goddess needs a name.

GOLDEN. So if you start to doubt that *you* can do it, you remember that *she* can.

NINA. I'm in a real band. I actually play the real guitar. So I'm not, you know, *super* worried about this. You guys seem like *really* invested, but how talented could anybody here tonight *really* be?

(They silently turn away from her and back to their beers.)

NINA. Oh, come on, don't be like that. Do you guys really take yourselves this seriously?

FACEBENDER. Ourselves, rarely. Air guitar, inevitably.

NINA. Well, shit. I didn't mean to insult anyone.

SHREDDY. *(not turning around)* We're not insulted. We just don't want to talk to you anymore.

NINA. You're just gonna ignore me for three hours? That's a long time.

GOLDEN. It will be for you.

(There is a seriously awkward pause. But FACEBENDER is not ready to give up on NINA yet.)

FACEBENDER. Miss, may I ask what drew you to our conclave this evening?

NINA. Conclave?

SHREDDY. Why did you register? Why are you here?

NINA. *(evasive)* It was kind of a spur-of-the-moment impulse. I was walking down the street yesterday and I saw a poster and I just . . . thought I'd see what this is all about.

FACEBENDER. We enthusiastically welcome all comers. But the first thing you must know is this: ours is not a community built upon competition, but camaraderie.

SHREDDY. There are a few dicks in the mix, but for the most part, everyone's chill.

NINA. I can be chill.

FACEBENDER. Do you swear it?

NINA. Swear.

SHREDDY. Okay then. Let's just see. What song are you performing?

NINA. Oh. Um, I thought I'd do "Don't Stop Believin'."

　　　(SHREDDY, GOLDEN, and FACEBENDER all groan in unison.)

SHREDDY. Are you serious right now?

NINA. What? It's an iconic song.

GOLDEN. Doesn't mean we want to hear it. *Again.*

SHREDDY. Not to mention the fact that the song doesn't exactly melt faces.

GOLDEN. Or deliver any kind of crucial message.

NINA. Neal Schon is a guitar prodigy! He played with Santana at fifteen!

SHREDDY. *(impressed)* Good point. Well made. But, the *song.* It just doesn't shred. And it doesn't have anything to do with you, unless you consider yourself just a small-town girl livin' in a lonely world. Journey is for stepmoms and frat boys. You have to play something that blasts *your soul,* Nina.

NINA. Fine, then I'll do "Sweet Child of Mine." You can't argue with the merits of that song.

SHREDDY. Slash himself has argued with the merits of that song. He started writing it as a string skipping guitar exercise.

NINA. And it ended up the band's best-charting song in the US.

GOLDEN. *(looking sidelong at SHREDDY)* Which is why everybody and his brother has already competed with it.

NINA. *(dismissive)* Look, I can play the Guns N' Roses song in my sleep. I don't have time to rehearse something new.

GOLDEN. If you pick the wrong song, rehearsal is kind of irrelevant, anyway.

NINA. *(annoyed)* Wow. Helpful. Thanks.

SHREDDY. A boring, overplayed, trite-ass song only works if your cut is subversive.

NINA. *(confused)* My . . . cut?

(The guys groan.)

SHREDDY. If you bomb up there, it's gonna bring down the quality of the show as a whole. I have like fifty different song cuts on my phone. Do you want to use one?

NINA. I'm good, thanks. I'm just gonna get up there and do what I do.

SHREDDY. But . . . this is not what you do.

NINA. Close enough.

(They shake their heads sadly.)

FACEBENDER. *(trying to find some hope for her)* Freestyle is merely the first round of competition. An exemplary score in the second round might be enough to propel you to victory. Since you are a musician, your technical prowess will aid you.

GOLDEN. And since you're local, you get two shots at Nationals. If you lose tonight, you can try again at the Eastern Conference Finals in a few months.

NINA. *(something occurs to her)* Wait, wait, you guys aren't from here?

FACEBENDER. San Diego.

SHREDDY. Chicago.

GOLDEN. Big Sky, Montana.

NINA. Y'all came from *out of state?* To *Staten Island?* For *air guitar?*

(There is a hostile silence.)

(The door opens, and CANNIBAL QUEEN *walks back in.* NINA *gasps and turns away.* CANNIBAL QUEEN *looks at her confused; she doesn't know who* NINA *is.)*

CANNIBAL QUEEN. *(pissed)* So Vicious has decided he can't be bothered to play the halftime show tonight.

GOLDEN. Aw, come on!

CANNIBAL QUEEN. Has anybody seen an organizer?

FACEBENDER. Maybe in the green room?

SHREDDY. What a dick-lick.

GOLDEN. Great. The crowd will be pissed off before I even get up there.

(CANNIBAL QUEEN exits to the green room.)

NINA. *(a little panicky)* He's still competing tonight, right? D Vicious?

SHREDDY. No. He was never gonna compete tonight.

NINA. But his name is on the poster!

SHREDDY. As the halftime entertainment. Vicious is the reigning champ. You're gonna have to make it all the way to nationals if you wanna face off against him.

(NINA is rethinking every decision that brought her to this moment. The lights shift into show mode.)

ANNOUNCER. Ladies and germs, welcome to your Staten Island Air Guitar qualifier! Since this is the home turf of our reigning National Champion, D Vicious, the Gods of Air have deigned to let us send tonight's winner all the way to Nationals! This is the last shot for those of you without a hometown semi-final, so I hope you're hungry!

(A bright, garish spotlight comes up onstage; NINA nervously moves into the light.)

NINA'S FIRST PERFORMANCE

(NINA stands onstage, ready. Nothing happens. FACEBENDER cues her from the audience to extend her arm and point her finger.)

[#2: "Sweet Child of Mine"]

(The intro of "Sweet Child of Mine" starts to play and NINA freezes.)

NINA. *(spiraling)* What are you doing here? Okay, hold the guitar. Fake guitar. Not-guitar. You can play it. You can play anything. You look like a damn fool and your parents would die of shame if they were in this bar right now, but you can play it. Breathe. You know the song. Don't freeze up. Just play the song.

(For an uncomfortable amount of time, NINA doesn't do anything to the music. Then she recovers, slightly, as we hear the crowd start to boo, bored. Finally, she plays the song as if she had a guitar in her hand, and it's accurate, but she seems miserable and she's not even looking at the crowd. Almost as soon as she finally begins

to play, the song is cut off. The sixty seconds are over. The small crowd boos, disinterested.)

FACEBENDER. *(from the bar)* Merciful God, is it over?

CANNIBAL QUEEN. *(from the bar)* Woof.

NINA. *(mortified)* Kill me. Somebody kill me.

(NINA is stuck onstage, mortified. GOLDEN approaches her and nudges her off the stage.)

GOLDEN. Please move aside. This crowd needs healing more than ever.

GOLDEN THUNDER'S PERFORMANCE

[#3: "The Supercut of Unity"]

(The Supercut of Unity begins to play—it is an epic mashup of "Johnny B. Goode" by Chuck Berry, "Rock Box" by Run DMC, and "Get By" by Talib Kweli.

The performance should include at least one costume change/ reveal.

GOLDEN gives an amazing air guitar performance. What he lacks in guitar-playing accuracy, he makes up in originality and interpretive glory. And he is the winner. Having to defend his art form to Nina has brought out a deeper level of artistry than he thought he had inside himself. His final costume change reveals a t-shirt that says "Make Air Not War," maybe in sequins.)

ANNOUNCER. All right, party people, the scores from both rounds are in! Taking first place here tonight in the Staten Island Qualifier, moving on to the National Finals, the man who puts the "art" in "farting around": Golden Thunder!

(Everyone onstage except NINA rallies around GOLDEN and cheers. NINA sees something that speaks to her. She's intrigued.

Lights dim on the bar in Staten Island.)

Vignette 1: Competition Videos

(A small light comes up on NINA *and* SHREDDY *with a laptop on the side of the stage. It is a few weeks later. They are watching old competition videos on the internet.* NINA *has a pen and a notepad.* SHREDDY *is holding out to her a single printed piece of paper.)*

SHREDDY. I'm just gonna need your John Hancock on this.

NINA. Oh come on. I told you I would buy all of your drinks—

SHREDDY. *(interrupting)* From now till Nationals.

NINA. From now till Nationals. And my word is good. We do not need a contract.

SHREDDY. Well, considering that you showed up in Staten Island outta nowhere, acted like a complete jerk to everybody, and then got up onstage and thoroughly annihilated yourself, you'll understand why I can't perform these services for you on the honor system. I'mma need you to sign this.

NINA. *(taking it from him and signing)* Fine. Whatever.

(He takes the contract from her, takes a picture of the paper, with his phone, then folds it up, and puts it in his pocket.)

SHREDDY. I'll email you a copy.

NINA. I'm good, thanks. *(short pause)* Do you do this for new people a lot?

SHREDDY. Sure. Anyone who asks.

NINA. That must take a lot of time.

SHREDDY. It does. But there's nothing else I'd rather be talking about, so.

NINA. And here I thought I was special.

SHREDDY. Well, I've never coached a girl before.

NINA. That's not reassuring.

SHREDDY. You signed a contract, lady. Let's begin.

NINA. Teach me. I have a notebook.

SHREDDY. We'll start with the foundation. You did the reading I sent you, yes?

NINA. Yes.

SHREDDY. Pop quiz! First round is—?

NINA. A sixty-second cut of a song I choose.

SHREDDY. Second round is—?

NINA. Sixty seconds of a song chosen by the judges.

SHREDDY. Points are given—?

NINA. On a scale of 4.0 to 6.0

SHREDDY. Exactly like—?

NINA. Figure skating.

SHREDDY. Optimum number of beers before a performance is—?

NINA. Two?

SHREDDY. *(makes a buzzer noise)* Eghnt! Three. This is known as the Monro Rule, discovered by and named after British champion -slash-air-guitar-god Zac Monro. Three beers.

NINA. Got it. Making a note.

SHREDDY. Now tell me: what are the six pillars of air guitar?

NINA. *(reading from her notebook)* Artistic merit, originality, feeling, technical ability, charisma, and airness.

SHREDDY. Great. Excellent. Memorize them. Internalize them. Metabolize them.

NINA. I don't know what any of that means.

SHREDDY. And *that* is why God invented YouTube. *(he types something into the computer)* Okay, okay, so this is the Portland qualifier, two years ago. This is a great place to start. It was a pretty small house, but everybody really tore it up that night.

> *(Three small squares of light come up in the middle of the stage.* FACEBENDER, CANNIBAL QUEEN, *and* GOLDEN *step into the boxes of light. They are in the videos. We watch them, and we see what* NINA *and* SHREDDY *are seeing.*
>
> NINA *and* SHREDDY *have the power to start and stop the videos, and the bodies of* FACEBENDER, CANNIBAL QUEEN, *and* GOLDEN *must respond accordingly.)*

SHREDDY. Okay, so here's our pal Golden Thunder. His highest marks are always in originality, as you saw in Staten Island, where he slayed.

NINA. Yeah. His whole unification theme was great.

SHREDDY. You picked up on that? I'm impressed.

NINA. He was wailing to an amazing supercut of songs with overt and covert political themes. What moron wouldn't put that together?

SHREDDY. Point Nina! Golden approached airness that night. There is no denying it. *(short pause)* We'll cover airness. Eventually.

NINA. One thing at a time.

SHREDDY. Obviously. So. As you'll see:

[#4: "Rebel Yell (Part 1)"]

(He presses "play" and GOLDEN comes to life. Billy Idol's "Rebel Yell" plays. GOLDEN rocks out for a few seconds. SHREDDY presses "pause," and GOLDEN freezes.)

SHREDDY. Golden's gift is that he can take a song that the judges have heard a hundred times, in this case "Rebel Yell", and make it totally his own, a brand new thing.

NINA. Looks pretty standard to me.

SHREDDY. Wait for it.

[#4: "Rebel Yell (Part 2)"]

(SHREDDY presses "play" again, and GOLDEN returns to rocking. After a few seconds, GOLDEN drops his pants, revealing boxer shorts he has created himself, that are half Confederate Flag, half Union Flag. GOLDEN shakes his fists at the sky. NINA hits "pause.")

NINA. Oh no.

SHREDDY. It's not over.

[#4: "Rebel Yell (Part 3)"]

(SHREDDY hits "play." GOLDEN rocks. After a moment, he fires a cannon and then plays guitar while writing. Fires another cannon. Shakes hands with himself. Finally, he drops his boxers and reveals a pair of American flag briefs. SHREDDY hits "pause.")

NINA. Was he writing the Emancipation Proclamation in the middle there?

SHREDDY. Very perceptive! And he fired cannons. And surrendered at Appomattox.

NINA. Amazing.

SHREDDY. Absolutely. Originality—you've got the idea.

NINA. Good stuff.

SHREDDY. Moving on! Facebender. What did I tell you in my email?

NINA. *(read from her notebook)* His highest marks are always for feeling.

SHREDDY. Exactly. In a lineup full of ego and testosterone and dudes grabbing their balls, Facebender is a bright spot of actual heart. He sends out his energy in a glorious wash over the crowd.

> [#5: *"More Than a Feeling"*]
>
> (SHREDDY *hits "play," and* FACEBENDER *comes to life. We hear the classic rock anthem from the 70s, "More Than a Feeling" by Boston.* FACEBENDER *plays, he feels, he doesn't move his hands much, but his face is a mask of emotion. He begins to cry, softly. It is so beautiful. It is also totally rock-n-roll.* NINA *hits "pause."* FACEBENDER *freezes.)*

NINA. Is he crying?

SHREDDY. He is.

NINA. It's . . . it's so beautiful.

SHREDDY. That dude uses air guitar to swim against a tide of real sadness. The judges see that. And they fucking respect it.

NINA. You can't fake that kind of heart.

SHREDDY. Exactly. You have to earn it. I gotta say, you're taking to this like a fish to water. *(short pause)* Now, Cannibal Queen—

> (CANNIBAL QUEEN *activates in her block of light, sensing her turn is next.)*

NINA. *(interrupting)* Nope. I don't want to watch her video.

> (CANNIBAL QUEEN *looks annoyed and disappointed.)*

SHREDDY. You can't just get up there and play whatever. It's not a dance routine. CQ is a classically trained guitarist, 100% about the music. Accuracy, specificity, and timing.

> (CANNIBAL QUEEN *gets ready to play.)*

NINA. The one thing I know is how to play guitar. Can we move on to the second round? My compulsory performance was almost as bad as my freestyle.

> (CANNIBAL QUEEN *deactivates, really annoyed now.)*

SHREDDY. Worse.

NINA. Hey!

SHREDDY. You seem to be kind of a natural, young padawan, so I'm not gonna sugarcoat anything for you.

NINA. Okay. Fair.

SHREDDY. *(short pause)* Now, your scores from Round One will be averaged with your scores from Round Two. For Round Two, as you experienced, it's harder to prepare.
Every finalist performs 60 seconds of a song picked by the judges. No one knows what the song will be ahead of time, so you have to be prepared for them to get really creative.

NINA. Creative how?

SHREDDY. Sometimes they pick a song that's super cliché, or super obscure. Sometimes they pick a song specifically to weed out the snobs. For instance, Louisville, four years ago.

> *[#6: "Take It Off"]*
>
> *(CANNIBAL QUEEN, FACEBENDER, and GOLDEN change places. SHREDDY hits "play." We hear "Take It Off" by The Donnas. CANNIBAL QUEEN, FACEBENDER, and GOLDEN all begin to play. After a moment, NINA hits "pause.")*

NINA. Who would dare to be snobby about The Donnas?

SHREDDY. Hair Metal Bros who don't understand that The Donnas are the spiritual successors to—

SHREDDY. *(in unison)* The Ramones.

NINA. *(in unison)* The Ramones.

SHREDDY. Yeah. Exactly.

> *(A moment of connection. Something *clicks* for both of them. NINA hits "play.")*
>
> *(CANNIBAL QUEEN, FACEBENDER, and GOLDEN all begin to play again. FACEBENDER is having a rough time. After a few seconds, SHREDDY hits "pause.")*

SHREDDY. You see how lost Facebender looks?

NINA. He's all over the place. That is in no way the shape or size of an actual guitar.

SHREDDY. Exactly. That was his first year. He had the heart and the drive, but he didn't have the mechanics. He totally tanked it. Plus, he had to go first. You want to go as late as you can, so you can hear the song a bunch of times. But, the later you go, the more original you have to be. Which is why Golden Thunder did better in this round.

NINA. Oh I can't wait.

(SHREDDY *presses "play." We hear "Take it Off."* GOLDEN *immediately takes his shirt off.* SHREDDY *presses "pause."*)

NINA. Really?

SHREDDY. I said he did better. I didn't say he did great. But Cannibal Queen—

(SHREDDY *hits "play." We hear "Take It Off," and* CANNIBAL QUEEN *slays. The sixty seconds finish.* NINA *hits "pause."* CANNIBAL QUEEN *has a huge grin on her face.*)

SHREDDY. Cannibal Queen takes it all.

NINA. *(darkly)* Yes. Yes she does.

(SHREDDY *looks her and raises his eyebrows.*)

NINA. *(avoiding a question she senses is coming)* Hey . . . in Staten Island. You're right, I was rude. I was really focused on winning and usually . . . usually the whole "lone wolf" thing works for me.

SHREDDY. We operate under more of a pack mentality.

NINA. I get that. It's cool. Anyway, I'm sorry if I offended you.

(Note: If SHREDDY *is played by an actor of color, omit the word "white" from the following line.)*

SHREDDY. *(shrugging)* Hey. I'm a straight white dude from the Midwest who doesn't believe in religion. It's kind of hard to offend me.

NINA. *(pause)* Han shot second.

SHREDDY. *(with gusto)* DIE IN A FIRE!

(Lights dim on the Vignette.)

Scene 2: San Diego, CA—Western Conference Finals

(Lights up on a larger, still dingy, bar in San Diego. It is two months after Staten Island. It is late afternoon, and there are no patrons here yet. GOLDEN *and* NINA *sit in the green room, drinking beers.)*

GOLDEN. To be perfectly frank, I'm impressed you came out tonight.

NINA. According to my research, I can still qualify for Nationals this year.

GOLDEN. If the Gods of Air are willing, you all can. Facebender's from San Diego, so he's got a good shot at the Western Conference title here tonight. Shreddy's hometown in Chicago, CQ's hometown in Boston, and you can make a comeback in New York.

NINA. *(quoting* GOLDEN*)* If the Gods of Air are willing.

GOLDEN. Thankfully, I gloriously triumphed in Staten Island. Because qualifiers are thin on the ground in Montana.

NINA. So this *(she motions to the bar)* is where the magic happens?

GOLDEN. Yes. This is where I touch the Divine.

NINA. Very cool. *(short pause)* You and Shreddy and everybody seem really close. Y'all hang out a lot?

GOLDEN. Nah. We're so spread out, we only see each other at competitions.

NINA. Bummer.

GOLDEN. But the group text is fire.

NINA. I'm sure.

GOLDEN. You gonna wow us onstage tonight? You can't qualify here, but you could work out some kinks, try some stuff out before NYC.

NINA. Uh, no. I'm doing recon.

GOLDEN. You don't need to take notes—you need to get back onstage. Air guitar is about the audience. The only way to really get better is to perform.

NINA. I know about audiences. What I don't know about is air guitar.

GOLDEN. You went down in flames in Staten Island. I know that had to sting like a motherfucker. But the longer you put off your comeback, the harder it's going to be to get back on that horse.

(NINA *is quiet.)*

NINA. I got lower scores than the guy who performed as resurrected Jesus.

GOLDEN. *(defensive)* To be fair, Pearl Jam's "Alive" was a strong artistic choice. If Jesus hadn't been drunk out of his mind, he might have swept the whole thing. *(pause)* So what are you working on for your comeback?

NINA. Got a couple things in the hopper. Tell me what you think.

GOLDEN. Okay.

(SHREDDY *enters behind them, unseen.)*

NINA. "Two Princes" by the Spin Doctors.

GOLDEN. Baby stuff.

NINA. The rhythm guitar part in that song is irresistible! Everybody loves that song!

GOLDEN. What else?

NINA. "Smells Like Teen Spirit."

GOLDEN. Okay, yeah, Nirvana is always a solid choice.

NINA. But?

GOLDEN. But what else you got, that's a little more original? That sends a message to the *crowd*, instead of being just fun for *you*?

NINA. Last but not least, I've been working on some choreo for "American Girl." Tom Petty.

> *(There are two possibilities for the following exchange. The second can be used if the actors playing NINA and GOLDEN are both actors of color, as they were in the original production.)*
>
> **(Option 1)**
>
> **GOLDEN.** *(unenthusiastic)* I get it.
>
> **NINA.** Because I'm . . . I'm an American girl. I guess.
>
> **GOLDEN.** No, no, it makes sense.
>
> **(Option 2)**
>
> **GOLDEN.** Were you raised by white people?
>
> **NINA.** Hey!
>
> **GOLDEN.** No, no, I get it.

NINA. But?

SHREDDY. *(piping up)* But, why are you the *only* person who could perform "American Girl"? Or "Smells Like Teen Spirit"? Or "Two Princes"? How is sixty seconds of one of those songs an extension of your soul, and *only your* soul?

NINA. Dude, how is "I Don't Wanna Grow Up" an extension of YOUR soul?

SHREDDY. Nina, that song is *my entire life*.

NINA. Yeah, yeah, yeah. How?

SHREDDY. You got bigger things to worry about than why I play what I play. What about your persona? Been working on that?

NINA. Oh yeah.

SHREDDY. And?

NINA. What do you think of *(putting on a British accent)* "Kate Middle Finger"?

SHREDDY. Who is she?

NINA. *(British accent)* My persona! *(she drops the accent)* It's like a play on the royal family.

SHREDDY. No one in the royal family plays rock guitar.

NINA. Okay, what about "Ruth Slayer Ginsburg." Get it? It's a pun!

SHREDDY. Is it?

GOLDEN. It's not the roller derby. You don't get points for puns.

NINA. Oh shut up. I think it's harder for girls. Who are my role models?

SHREDDY. Cannibal Queen.

NINA. I hate that cunt.

SHREDDY / GOLDEN. *(in unison, interrupting)* Whoa!

SHREDDY. What is that *language* about? Did CQ do something to you?

NINA. Fuck off.

(They wait. She clams up.)

GOLDEN. Well, fine, because now that Shreddy's here, I have some gossip for the group. Guess what I heard. Guess.

SHREDDY. Um . . .

GOLDEN. You won't guess. *(dramatic pause)* Facebender's kid is coming tonight!

SHREDDY. Facebender has a KID?

GOLDEN. Yeah, a daughter, he had her when he was like sixteen. And he always invites her to the San Diego finals, and she never comes. Until *tonight,* you guys.

NINA. Whoa.

GOLDEN. Yeah. Whoa. So we gotta do everything we can to pump up the crowd. His charisma marks have to be off the charts.

(SHREDDY points to NINA to prompt her to recite a lesson he has taught her about charisma.)

NINA. *(proud of herself)* Oooh! It doesn't matter if the crowd loves you or hates you, as long as they're making a lot of noise. Like TV wrestling!

SHREDDY. *(proud of* NINA*)* Exactly, Grasshopper.

GOLDEN. Charisma marks are always high for villains. Cannibal Queen, for one—

SHREDDY. *(interrupting, to* NINA*)* Your fave gal. We're gonna come back to that, by the way.

GOLDEN. *(continuing)* And D Vicious, who won the National Championship last year. He does this thing where he makes the crowd love him, then hate him, then love him again. In sixty seconds. Surely you've seen his routine?

NINA. Oh. I've seen it. Up close.

GOLDEN. But Facebender's not a villain. He's like . . . your sad uncle . . .

SHREDDY. . . . from another century, or a story . . . or . . .

NINA. He's Don Quixote. A man out of time. He dreams the impossible dream.

SHREDDY. *(nodding in agreement)* Uh-huh.

NINA. Is he gonna play "Simple Man" for the freestyle round again?

GOLDEN. He's been playing it all season.

NINA. That's why he hasn't qualified yet.

(SHREDDY *and* GOLDEN *look at her sideways, affronted on their friend's behalf.*)

NINA. He's Don Quixote, playing, like, a Huckleberry Finn song.

GOLDEN. She's right. I'm impressed.

SHREDDY. Nina's got a great eye for what's going on under the hood of a routine.

NINA. *(smiling at* SHREDDY*)* I have a good coach.

(FACEBENDER *enters. Very nervous.*)

GOLDEN. Facebender Lender! Don't be nervous! This is your night, my dude!

FACEBENDER. You are a true and loyal friend, Golden Thunder. I wish I shared your optimism.

SHREDDY. We heard about your daughter, man.

GOLDEN. I told them. Hope it wasn't a secret.

FACEBENDER. A secret? Indeed no. My . . . my Sophia. She's never seen me play before. I haven't always been . . . the ideal patriarch. Of our little kingdom.

GOLDEN. And you're gonna melt her face off!

(*They all look at him sideways.*)

GOLDEN. Nope. Weird to say about a man's daughter. Now I say it, I hear it.

SHREDDY. She's gonna love it. How old is she? Doesn't matter. She's gonna love it.

FACEBENDER. (*dropping the façade for a moment*) I can't fuck this up in front of my kid. The only way this is anything at all is if I'm good at it. If it's not balls-out amazing, I'm . . . I'm just . . . I've already let her down a thousand times.

GOLDEN. Hey? Hey, Facebender? What are you always telling me?

FACEBENDER. To take the threat of alcohol poisoning more seriously.

GOLDEN. No. Yes. No. What are you always telling me when I start to doubt my badassitude? Huh, buddy? What's the greatest thing about air guitar?

NINA. Oh, I wanna know this.

GOLDEN. What does air guitar teach? (*pause*) "Everything we need to rock, is already inside us."

(SHREDDY *and* FACEBENDER *nod sagely.* NINA *is moved, unexpectedly.*)

FACEBENDER. (*recovering his persona somewhat*) The greatest truth of this, our chosen art form. Sage of you to remind me, Golden Thunder. But . . . I have a dread in my bones.

NINA. A dread?

FACEBENDER. A real dread. That the ode I have selected for my freestyle contribution, will do me no favors. It has won me no accolades thus far. Why should I expect it to triumph this night?

NINA. You think the song will fail you?

FACEBENDER. Or I, the song. And my Sophia.

(CANNIBAL QUEEN *enters. She has the worst timing. She looks at their anxious faces.*)

CANNIBAL QUEEN. Ugh. Who died in here?

FACEBENDER. Cannibal Queen, even your lovely disposition cannot retrieve me from the funk into which I have fallen. But thank you for trying.

CANNIBAL QUEEN. Yeah sure. My pleasure. *(looking around)* Has anyone seen Vicious?

(*NINA inhales sharply.*)

SHREDDY. He coming tonight?

CANNIBAL QUEEN. Maybe. He said he might.

GOLDEN. *(teasing)* Aw, you need your BF to hold your hand? Since you haven't qualified yet?

CANNIBAL QUEEN. Next week. Boston. Home turf. Mark my fuckin' words, I'm going home with first. And Vicious is not my BF. I'm married, for Chrissake. He's just, we're just, whatever.

NINA. You're married?!

CANNIBAL QUEEN. Who are you, again? I'm usually the only vagina in the room.

NINA. I'm . . . um . . .

SHREDDY. She's still working on a persona.

NINA. The . . .

SHREDDY. She's not competing again until NYC, so she has some time.

NINA. Nina!

CANNIBAL QUEEN. The Nina? Are you backed by the Pinta and the Santa Maria?

NINA. The Nina.

GOLDEN. Righteous. I love that.

CANNIBAL QUEEN. It has . . . a ring. I guess. Cool. Anyways, if any of you see D Vicious, tell him I'm looking for him.

SHREDDY. Your "not-boyfriend."

GOLDEN. With whom you "just whatever."

CANNIBAL QUEEN. Exactly.

(*CANNIBAL QUEEN exits. NINA looks at SHREDDY, almost frantically.*)

NINA. He's not really going to be here tonight, is he? David Cooper?

GOLDEN. She knows his *full* name.

SHREDDY. Let me guess, you saw his Sprite commercial.

NINA. No. I mean, yes, I saw it, I just . . . do you really think he'll be here?

(FACEBENDER *slowly and sadly begins to remove his wig.*)

SHREDDY. Probably not. He hasn't come to a single qualifier this year, and he bailed on that Staten Island halftime show. That dude used to be a friend, but now he's just . . .

NINA. The competition?

SHREDDY. *(bitterly)* Yeah.

GOLDEN. *(looking over at* FACEBENDER*)* Aw, Facebender, man, put your wig back on!

FACEBENDER. *(teetering on the edge)* What is the point, my friends? Shall I disgrace myself and dishonor Lynyrd Skynyrd on the same night, in front of my only progeny?

SHREDDY. *(sighing)* What?

GOLDEN. He's still conflicted about "Simple Man."

NINA. *(taking charge)* Okay, Facebender, look me in the eyes. Take a deep breath in, now hold it, now a deep breath out. Good. Now another deep breath in, hold it, aaaand out. You're doing great.

SHREDDY. What are you, like a first responder?

NINA. Nope. I'm a web developer. And I'm about to troubleshoot the shit outta this situation.

FACEBENDER. I put myself entirely in your hands, The Nina.

NINA. We have four hours till the show. Plenty of time for you to choreograph a performance for a new song, IF it's the right song. And IF we all contribute.

SHREDDY. I'm in.

GOLDEN. Whatever I can do to help, Bender Buddy.

(NINA *begins to pace, thinking on her feet. They all watch her.*)

NINA. Okay. First let's consider our audience. What do West Coast people like?

FACEBENDER. Sunshine!

SHREDDY. Driving with the top down and the music blasting!

GOLDEN. Almonds! *(off their looks)* What? They do! They all eat organic food and drink green juice and almonds are like, part of that.

NINA. Okay, so what we're circling around here, is a culture of people, including you, Bender, who like the sun, and wind in their hair, and who want to live forever.

FACEBENDER. Yes. Yes!

NINA. And then, there's a special person in the room. There's a specific, special person in the audience that you want to reach, even more than the judges, isn't there? How do you reach her? What is the song that feels like sunshine, that speaks directly from you to her?

SHREDDY. We find that song, and it'll play right to your strengths.

GOLDEN. Oh, this is some voodoo.

NINA. No. It's targeted advertising. It's not about whether or not the judges "get" it. It's about the magic in the crowd.

GOLDEN. She's right, 'Bender. If you can grab Sophia by the soul, the judges will have no choice but to go along for the ride.

NINA. You're her father. What's the sound?

FACEBENDER. *(he finds the song inside himself)* Oh! OH, my comrades. There is a song. I know it. And it slays.

> **FACEBENDER'S PERFORMANCE**
>
> *(Lights shift quickly and* GOLDEN, EDDY, CANNIBAL QUEEN, FACEBENDER, *and* NINA *appear, lined up across the bar's stage, under the bright lights of the show. We hear a sound cue of a medium-sized, but enthusiastic, cheering crowd.)*
>
> **[#7: "Keep On Loving You"]**
>
> *(*FACEBENDER *steps out in front of the other characters as sixty seconds of REO Speedwagon's "Keep on Loving You" begin to play.*
>
> FACEBENDER *is the perfect combination of bombastic and vulnerable. He is laying it all on the line. He's found the perfect song to convey how much he loves his daughter [Did he used to sing this to her as a baby?] and how hard he rocks at the same time. He's a luminous success, basking in how hard he's feeling it, and the judges can't deny the power of that.)*

ANNOUNCER. People, I am thrilled to announce, in first place here tonight at the Western Conference Finals, moving on to the National Championship, the man who ain't ashamed to rock with his heart on his sleeve: FACEBENDER!

NINA. *(to* SHREDDY*)* What do you get if you win the World Championships, anyway?

SHREDDY. Limited-edition custom Flying Finn electric guitar.

NINA. A REAL GUITAR?? A real guitar is the grand prize??

SHREDDY. *(shrugging)* What?

(Lights dim on the bar in San Diego.)

Scene 3: Boston, MA—Mid-Atlantic Conference Finals

(Lights up on a medium-sized, still dingy, bar in Boston. It is the next week. It is late afternoon, and there are no patrons here yet.

NINA sits in the green room, drinking a beer and working on her computer. This goes on in silence for a moment, until CANNIBAL QUEEN enters.)

CANNIBAL QUEEN. Oh, good, you're here. The Nina, right? I wanna talk to you.

NINA. *(a little panicky)* What? Why? Can't you see I'm working?

(Genuinely curious, CANNIBAL QUEEN gets momentarily derailed from her original purpose.)

CANNIBAL QUEEN. What kind of work can you do from the back of a shitty bar?

NINA. *(hostile)* I build websites. I can do it from anywhere.

CANNIBAL QUEEN. Oh. Cool. You don't have to quit your job for the season.

NINA. People quit their jobs to play air guitar?

CANNIBAL QUEEN. Yeah, that's half the fun. There's always another bartending job. Or an Uber to drive. No one's leaving their job at the Pentagon or anything.

NINA. And what job did you quit to be here tonight?

CANNIBAL QUEEN. I've got a Masters in classical guitar. So, I mean, I guess I'll teach eventually, when I'm like fifty. Mostly right now, I just do air guitar. And I'm married.

NINA. So it's *his* money that keeps you in leather pants and hair extensions?

CANNIBAL QUEEN. Number one, this is my real hair. Number two, yes, it's his money, and he doesn't care what I do with it as long as I'm happy. *(refocusing)* And number three—I want to talk to you, woman-to-woman. I can really help you, you know. If more of us, who are competent, join the circuit, eventually they'll have to let one of us win.

NINA. I don't want your help.

CANNIBAL QUEEN. You one-a those bitches who can't be friends with other girls?

NINA. I'm friends with plenty of girls.

CANNIBAL QUEEN. Good. So let's get down to business. I don't know what the scarecrow, the tin man, and the lion have been telling you, but it's different for us. You have to be really careful not to give the crowd everything.

NINA. What does that even mean?

CANNIBAL QUEEN. Don't let them use you as entertainment.

NINA. Entertainment?

CANNIBAL QUEEN. Okay, so like, costume for one thing. You'll see girls who do the whole short skirt, pigtails, fuck-me boots thing— they never win. The organizers love when they enter, because they give the crowd something to drool over. But they never place. They'll tell you to smile, jump around, flash your tits, but don't listen to that bullshit. I don't give them anything but the music. You have to fight for every second of stage time, and that starts with not dressing like a prostitute.

(NINA *is silent.* CANNIBAL QUEEN *decides to continue being helpful, in her own special way.*)

CANNIBAL QUEEN. And you need a better song. Your freestyle round in Staten Island was nonsense.

NINA. I'm working on something new.

CANNIBAL QUEEN. What?

NINA. Heart.

CANNIBAL QUEEN. Heart?! Oh, barf. Come on, it's so cliché.

NINA. *(very defensive)* Hey, Nancy Wilson's guitar playing basically defined the sound of the 70s and 80s. *(short pause)* But I'm also working on some Joan Jett.

CANNIBAL QUEEN. Jesus. You don't have to do a female guitarist because you're a girl. If you want to play with the boys, think like the boys.

NINA. Or, you know, think for yourself.

CANNIBAL QUEEN. Yeah, just don't give them any excuse to write you off, is all I'm saying. If you're gonna do this, actually *do it*. The right way.

NINA. Joan Jett made me want to play guitar! *(short pause)* Anyway, why do you care? Why are you lecturing me?

CANNIBAL QUEEN. This is how mean people make friends—we instruct.

NINA. You and I are not gonna be friends.

CANNIBAL QUEEN. What is your damage?

NINA. You're married! You're married, and you're fucking Da— D Vicious. Aren't you?

CANNIBAL QUEEN. Ooooooh. Are you a fangirl? Are you a little D Vicious fangirl?

NINA. *(short pause)* No. I'm his fiancée.

CANNIBAL QUEEN. WHAT?!

NINA. Or. I was.

CANNIBAL QUEEN. Oh, no. Fuck me. Hey! I didn't know he had a fiancée! He never told me.

(NINA is not expecting to hear this, and it throws her for a moment.)

NINA. W-would you have cared if he had told you?

CANNIBAL QUEEN. Yes. YES. I don't poach.

NINA. You cheat on your husband.

CANNIBAL QUEEN. Not that it's any of your business, but ethical non-monogamy is an *established* part of our marriage. It doesn't mean I go around scamming on other girls' dudes.

NINA. Well. You scammed on mine. And you still are, aren't you? You're still dating him.

CANNIBAL QUEEN. Hey, I'm sorry a shitty thing happened to you, but this bad blood is between you and Vicious. Leave me out of it.

(The door to the green room opens, and VICIOUS enters.)

CANNIBAL QUEEN. Oh, Christ.

(VICIOUS moves to CANNIBAL QUEEN first, not looking at NINA. He tries to kiss her on the cheek.)

VICIOUS. Hey, gorgeous.

CANNIBAL QUEEN. *(pulling away, nodding her head at NINA)* Nope.

VICIOUS. *(seeing NINA)* Fucking hell. Nina?!

NINA. It's The Nina now.

VICIOUS. What? What the fuck are you doing here?

CANNIBAL QUEEN. And that's my cue to find another place to be.

(CANNIBAL QUEEN exits.)

VICIOUS. *(calling after her)* Astrid? ASTRID?! *(Wheeling around to NINA)* What is this, some kind of ambush?

NINA. Oh, calm down. It's not an ambush. I didn't even know you'd be in Boston.

VICIOUS. I'm the reigning National Champion. I could be anywhere.

NINA. I haven't seen you at any of the other qualifiers.

VICIOUS. How many of these competitions have you been to?

NINA. All of them. All over. Facebender's victory in San Diego last week? I was there. I helped him pick his new song. We're *friends* now.

VICIOUS. Stop. Stop talking. You made fun of me, you bitched at me, for a *solid year* for playing air guitar. And now you're suddenly *on* the circuit?

NINA. My persona is "The Nina."

VICIOUS. THAT'S THE STUPIDEST NAME I'VE EVER HEARD. *(a realization)* Are you—are you trying to get me back?

NINA. No.

VICIOUS. This is about my Sprite commercial, isn't it?

NINA. NO! That stupid commercial was only online, anyway! And nobody likes Sprite!

VICIOUS. People fucking LOVE Sprite!

NINA. You didn't win the goddamn Nobel Prize!

VICIOUS. And yet, you're following me. You never wanted me to do this, you made fun of me to your friends, your parents, anyone who would listen, you NEVER came to a SINGLE show, but now that I'm the champion, oh, suddenly, here you are. Now you care, and you're at every qualifier. I'm suspicious, I gotta tell you. But, fuck it, I shouldn't be. You can't just be supportive, you always know better.

NINA. Oh, I have problems with being supportive? Says the guy who bailed out of nowhere.

VICIOUS. Oh, yeah. We had a perfect relationship and no problems and I just bolted. Sure, you go ahead and tell yourself that.

NINA. I came home one day, and all your stuff was gone. No call, no note, just "You Give Love a Bad Name" blaring on repeat.

VICIOUS. There was no point in having another fight when you had stopped listening.

NINA. When you started to get good at air guitar, you checked out of our relationship.

VICIOUS. Maybe I did, Nina. Because I suddenly remembered what it was like to be around people who *wanted to be around me.*

NINA. I loved you! I loved our band and our apartment and our life. I loved you.

VICIOUS. It was impossible to feel that. *(short pause)* I don't want our old life, and I don't want you. You're fucking awful.

NINA. *(discovering this)* Oh, this is your *favorite.* This moment when I feel stupid and say too much and you have all the power. You *love* this.

VICIOUS. Oh, that is so typically your shit. You act like you don't need help from anybody, but blame everyone else when you fail.

(A hit. A palpable hit.)

NINA. *(pause)* I'm not doing this to get you back.

(Unseen by NINA, GOLDEN, FACEBENDER, and SHREDDY enter the green room. As soon as they see what's happening they stop short, and quietly eavesdrop.)

VICIOUS. Then why are you here, Nina??

NINA. Because. When someone breaks your heart, you find out what they love most in the whole world. Then you take it from them.

VICIOUS. *(short pause)* You are very dark inside.

NINA. You're damn right. And whose fault is that?

VICIOUS. Your terrible parents?

NINA. You broke up our REAL band, you broke up our REAL relationship, for what? To fuck somebody else's wife and spend every night in shitty bars with people who think you're cool because you're the best at IMAGINARY GUITAR? To play PRETEND with a gaggle of second-rate UNFUCKABLE LOSERS who couldn't be contributing members of society if they tried? THIS is your kingdom? THIS is where you're god? You ruined my REAL LIFE, and you get to be happy in PRETEND LAND? FUCK THAT, and FUCK YOU. It may be shitty, it may be imaginary, but I'm here to take it from you.

(VICIOUS nods his head in the direction of the new arrivals. No one says anything. NINA *is mortified;* SHREDDY, GOLDEN, *and* FACEBENDER *are crestfallen.)*

VICIOUS. Yeah. Good luck with that. *(short pause)* See you in New York.

(VICIOUS exits. NINA *turns to her friends, desperate to apologize.)*

NINA. Guys! GUYS! I didn't mean that stuff, I didn't! He gets into my head. Please!

(They brush past her and take positions at the front of the stage.)

SHREDDY. *(without looking at her)* Whatever, Nina.

CANNIBAL QUEEN'S PERFORMANCE

(Lights shift quickly. GOLDEN, SHREDDY, FACEBENDER, *and* NINA *appear, lined up across the bar's stage, under the bright lights of the show. They are joined downstage by* CANNIBAL QUEEN *and* VICIOUS. *We hear a sound cue of a medium-sized, but enthusiastic, cheering crowd. There is also a fair amount of booing in the mix, but that's okay;* CANNIBAL QUEEN's *persona is a villain.)*

ANNOUNCER. Well, well, well! Ladies and gentlemen, chalk one up for the Women's Movement! Taking home the gold tonight here in Boston, and repping the Mid-Atlantic region at Nationals next month, your hometown heroine, the lady we all hate to love: CANNIBAL QUEEN!

(The crowd cheers.)

ANNOUNCER. What's that? What's that?? Hey Cannibal Queen, your subjects want a fuckin' encore!

[#8: "Arpeggios From Hell"]

(CANNIBAL QUEEN steps out in front of the other characters and absolutely shreds a classically-inspired rock track with no lyrics, "Arpeggios From Hell" by Yngwie Malmsteen.

CANNIBAL QUEEN *is technically flawless, with the concentration of a surgeon. She isn't flashy. She gives the audience nothing but the music; but the music, and her facility with it, is astonishing. It is by far the most technically difficult song of the competition, and she doesn't miss a single note. She also doesn't smile. When she's done, she takes a brisk, curt bow, like a concert pianist, then stands up straight and flips off the audience with both middle fingers. They go wild with boos.)*

(VICIOUS walks up to CANNIBAL QUEEN *and plants a huge kiss on her lips.* GOLDEN, SHREDDY, *and* FACEBENDER *gather around* CANNIBAL QUEEN *to congratulate her. Everyone except* NINA *exits together, celebrating.* NINA *is alone onstage, looking miserable.*

Lights dim on the bar in Boston.)

If you need to take an intermission, it goes here.

Vignette 2: D Vicious's Sprite Commercial

(A small light comes up on NINA, *hunched over a laptop or her phone on the side of the stage. It is a few days later. She is watching the outtakes of D Vicious's Sprite commercial on the internet.*

Over the course of this Vignette, we will see how D Vicious went from an enthusiastic lover of the sport of air guitar, to the jaded buzzkill he is today. The outtakes of this commercial are a microcosm of his past year. In the first take, he is ten times happier than we've seen him. In the final take, he's the man we now know.

VICIOUS *enters; he is in his full persona and costume.)*

[#9: "Crowd Chant"]

(We hear an amped up crowd-pleaser played, Joe Satriani's "Crowd Chant," as VICIOUS *runs around the stage performing. He's exuberant. He works the crowd like a master, using the song's built-in call-and-response. After 30-45 seconds, the song cuts off abruptly.*

We hear the SPRITE EXEC's *voice [but we don't see him/her], which seems to come from everywhere.)*

SPRITE EXEC. So what am I watching here?

VICIOUS. This is something new I'm working on. "Crowd Chant." Joe Satriani? I have a few other cuts on my phone, too, if you want to see something different.

SPRITE EXEC. "Cum on Feel the Noize." That's what we want to see.

VICIOUS. But, I won Nationals with that song.

SPRITE EXEC. Exactly. And that's why we hired you.

VICIOUS. But everyone's already seen me do that song.

SPRITE EXEC. Look, if it works, work it. Don't mess with success, kid.

VICIOUS. But—

SPRITE EXEC. And stay in your box.

VICIOUS. My box?

(A small square of light comes up in the middle of the stage.)

SPRITE EXEC. Your mark. Stay on your mark, genius. Look down.

(VICIOUS looks down at the little box of light on the floor.)

VICIOUS. Oh. Um, okay.

SPRITE EXEC. Let's take it from the line. We'll just dub "Cum on Feel the Noize" over whatever he just did.

VICIOUS. Hey, I can—!

SPRITE EXEC. *(interrupting)* David Cooper Sprite commercial, take two.

(VICIOUS centers himself and regains most of his enthusiasm. He takes a big sip from an imaginary can of Sprite.)

VICIOUS. *(holding an imaginary can)* Take it from me, D Vicious: Sprite will *slay* your thirst!

(VICIOUS does a mean air guitar lick, and looks deliriously happy to be here.)

SPRITE EXEC. Okay, lose the air drinking.

VICIOUS. But it's funny!

SPRITE EXEC. Is it?

VICIOUS. Because I'm an air guitar champion.

SPRITE EXEC. Stick to the script, please.

(VICIOUS looks annoyed. He resets.)

SPRITE EXEC. David Cooper Sprite commercial, take ten.

VICIOUS. Take it from me, D Vicious: Sprite will *slay* your thirst!

(VICIOUS does a sick power slide across the stage. Stands up. Looks defiant and pleased.)

SPRITE EXEC. Don't do that.

VICIOUS. Come on, man! The power slide is my signature move.

SPRITE EXEC. You slid right out of frame.

VICIOUS. Well, follow me!

SPRITE EXEC. Stick to your blocking. This is not hard, here, "champ."

VICIOUS. *(crestfallen)* Whatever.

> *(VICIOUS is chastised. He resets.)*

SPRITE EXEC. David Cooper Sprite commercial, take fourteen.

VICIOUS. Take it from me, D Vicious: Sprite will *slay* your thirst!

> *(VICIOUS does a sweet double crane kick.)*

SPRITE EXEC. *(weary)* No power slides. No karate. No finger guns. No twirling. No death drops. No air guitar. Just say the line and look at the camera. Got it?

VICIOUS. COME ON!

SPRITE EXEC. Reset!

> *(VICIOUS is livid. He resets.)*

SPRITE EXEC. *(wearier still)* David Cooper Sprite commercial, take twenty-five.

VICIOUS. *(grumpily)* Take it from me, D Vicious: *(he steps halfway out of his box of light)* Sprite will—

SPRITE EXEC. *(interrupting)* You're off your mark.

VICIOUS. *(stepping back into the light, flipping up both middle fingers)* Go fuck yourself!

> *(VICIOUS storms off. NINA closes the laptop. She's actually feeling bad for Vicious, and she doesn't want to.)*

NINA. *(sympathetic, in spite of herself)* Damn. Damn it.

> *(NINA exits.*
> *Lights dim on the Vignette.)*

Scene 4: Chicago, IL—Central Conference Finals

> *(Lights up on a large, but still dingy, bar in Chicago. Somewhere like The Metro. It is the next week. It is late afternoon, and there are no patrons here yet.)*

> *(NINA sits alone at the bar, nursing a beer. She got here very, very early. She wanted to catch people coming in the door.*
> *She waits. Eventually, FACEBENDER walks in.)*

NINA. Bender! Facebender! Over here!

FACEBENDER. Ah. The Nina. *(pause, he turns to go)* If you'll excuse me.

(NINA *stands and blocks his way.*)

NINA. Please! Stay. I want to apologize. Did you get my messages?

FACEBENDER. I did. Thank you so much for your remorseful sentiments. *(pause)* I must to the green room now.

NINA. I apologized! Now forgive me!

FACEBENDER. *(dropping his façade)* You called us "second-rate unfuckable losers."

NINA. I was out of my mind.

FACEBENDER. When we come to these competitions, it's OUR space, get it? It might smell like old sweat and stale beer in here, but it's supposed to be safe.

NINA. I didn't mean all that stuff you heard me say to David. That wasn't the real me! He . . . he turns me into a rage monster. It's really gnarly. It's like I took a time machine right back to our breakup. But I'm not that person anymore, I promise. I'm a million times sorry, okay?

(FACEBENDER *is unconvinced.*)

NINA. Hey, remember San Diego? Remember when I calmed you down, and we all worked as, like, a kickass squad, and then you absolutely slayed? And then you added me to the group text? That's the real me. That's The Nina.

(FACEBENDER *regards her for a moment, then relents. His demeanor softens. His façade is still dropped.*)

FACEBENDER. Do you want to know how I got into air guitar?

NINA. I would love to know.

(*During this speech,* FACEBENDER *walks behind the bar and grabs himself a beer, before joining* NINA *in front of the bar again.*)

FACEBENDER. I work for the County of San Diego.

NINA. What do you do? None of you ever talk about your jobs.

FACEBENDER. Because when we're here, everything outside is irrelevant. Except for right now, when I'm telling you this story.

NINA. Got it.

FACEBENDER. Do you know what a Public Guardian is?

NINA. Like . . . Batman?

FACEBENDER. *(laughing)* No. Nothing like Batman. If a person, usually a poor person, dies, and there's no family or friends or will that can be located, somebody still has to clean out their apartment, and bury their body, and tie up their loose ends. That's my job. The apartment-cleaning bit.

NINA. Whoa. How do you get a job like that?

(Note: During the following monologue, it's important that FACEBENDER does not feel sorry for himself at all. These are the facts of his reality, and communicating them to NINA will make her understand why air guitar is vital.)

FACEBENDER. Well, it was a match made in heaven. Nobody wants that job, and at the time, nobody wanted me. I was bumming around, couldn't find anything steady. Had run up some sizeable debts. I heard about this job from a buddy, and it sounded easy enough, so I applied. And I got it. You basically just have to be willing to walk into disgusting apartments.

Sometimes we have to wear hazmat suits and bootees. These people can be dead for weeks, or months, before anyone finds them. Before anyone cares. Sometimes there are flies, or roaches, or mice. Lots of times, people's apartments are just full of wall-to-wall junk. This one lady last year, died standing up and stayed that way. There wasn't room in her place to fall over.

We work in pairs, to keep us from stealing. It's weird, seeing what strangers kept in their closets, what they ate, what movies they watched, what kind of toilet paper they used. We go through everything, looking for signs of relationships. Is there an address book? A business card? A computer? Who are the people in these photographs? Are they still alive, would they care that this person is dead? It's the most depressing kind of archeology, but somebody has to do it. And that somebody in San Diego County has been me, for the last few years. I've been through a lot of partners. But I'll tell you one thing.

NINA. *(rapt)* What?

FACEBENDER. When I die, somebody is gonna know. Right away. Lots of people. I used to go through my life like I was gonna live forever, but now I know. It could be any day. But I won't go out anonymous. No stranger is going to have to pick through my stuff, wondering if there's anybody out in the world who'd care to inherit the $300 in my bank account. Before I started playing air guitar, I hadn't seen my daughter, or her mother, in like six years. I felt like too much time had passed, and I was embarrassed to reach out to them. Now, we hang out at least once a month. It's awkward as fuck, but it's happening. It's getting there.

(Unseen by NINA *and* FACEBENDER, GOLDEN *and* SHREDDY *enter the bar.)*

FACEBENDER. My list of friends gets longer and longer. I text them every day. I hug them every time I see them. When I die, there are gonna be so many broken-hearted motherfuckers playing sad, sad air guitar solos at my funeral. I put it in my will.

NINA. That's amazing.

FACEBENDER. I look death in its nasty face every day. And then at night, I come here, and I get up onstage and *live* like there's no tomorrow. Because there isn't. There really isn't. It's silly and it's fun and it's absurd, but life is a slow march off a cliff into nothingness, so why not be as silly as you want?

GOLDEN. I'm gonna play "Stairway to Heaven" at your funeral. All eight minutes and three seconds. Got my routine all worked out.

SHREDDY. I was thinking Weezer's "Say It Ain't So." Some strong power chords to carry you into the next life.

FACEBENDER. *(resuming his persona)* Gentlemen, Miss The Nina is heartily sorry for her offenses in Boston. I move that we unanimously accept her sincere apology.

NINA. I'm so, so, SO, SO SORRY. I'm the worst. I know.

SHREDDY. Lots of people want to fuck us, actually.

GOLDEN. And we ARE contributing members of society. This all might be pretend, but it's serious pretend.

NINA. I get it. Can I please get back on the group text? PLEASE?

*(*GOLDEN, FACEBENDER, *and* SHREDDY *exchange looks.)*

SHREDDY. What do you say, guys?

GOLDEN. *(shrugging)* Ah, hell.

FACEBENDER. I believe the standard ritual of reconciliation will serve as a suitable penance.

(The three men turn to look at NINA.*)*

NINA. Which is?

(The three men walk over to NINA *and, one by one, very specifically, they "lean" their air guitars against the bar in front of her.)*

SHREDDY. Tune our guitars.

NINA. Oh, COME ON!

GOLDEN. Tune them! That shows us you're truly sorry!

FACEBENDER. It is the traditional mode.

NINA. *(grumbling)* Fine.

SHREDDY. Do mine first, since I'm competing.

>(NINA *"picks up" the "guitar" that* SHREDDY *put down, and begins to tune it as she would a real guitar. He watches her to make sure she's really doing it.)*

SHREDDY. Much obliged.

>(NINA *tunes the air guitars until they are all ready, however long that takes.)*

NINA. *(grumbling good-naturedly)* This is a bit much, y'all.

GOLDEN. Ah-ah-ah! If you think you're too good to be here, the judges can smell it a mile away. Mockery is the enemy of airness.

FACEBENDER. Sir, have you just created that glorious motto in this moment?

GOLDEN. Sure did.

FACEBENDER. Extraordinary!

GOLDEN. I thank you.

NINA. Okay, how many of these things do I have to watch before I understand what airness is?

GOLDEN. One never understands airness. One ACHIEVES airness.

SHREDDY. It can't be coached. It almost can't be explained.

NINA. Oh, that clears it up.

SHREDDY. I'll tell you what airness is NOT. Airness is NOT taking notes on what everyone is doing, but never getting up onstage to try anything yourself.

GOLDEN. VERY true.

FACEBENDER. In our world, Miss The Nina, the life of the spectator and the life of the performer are two halves of the same whole. You cannot fully appreciate one without the other.

NINA. I'll get there, okay? Next month? New York? I'll be so ready.

GOLDEN. New York is a huge venue and the competition will be fierce as hell.

NINA. *(slightly annoyed)* I'll know when I'm ready. Trust me.

SHREDDY. *(doubtful)* Okay. It's just way more fun if you actually play.

(They all nod. NINA looks uncomfortable. The door opens, and CANNIBAL QUEEN sticks her head in. Seeing who's in the room, she scurries as fast as she can through the bar and exits to the green room, without saying a word to anyone.)

FACEBENDER. *(softly, to himself, but GOLDEN overhears)* Why does she run from me?

GOLDEN. Dude, that was most definitely not about you.

(FACEBENDER follows CANNIBAL QUEEN off into the green room, and GOLDEN follows FACEBENDER. NINA and SHREDDY are alone. It's the tiniest bit awkward.)

NINA. Shreddy, I really am sorry.

SHREDDY. You said. You tuned.

NINA. Yeah, but I feel like I should . . . I need to say something more. To you. You were nice enough to coach me and I felt like maybe we were becoming . . . like . . . maybe . . .

SHREDDY. Is it that hard for you to say the word "friends"?

NINA. *(jokingly confused)* Fa-rends? Yes, friends. I want us to be friends because I think you're cool.

SHREDDY. I am. I am cool.

(A short pause. He smiles at her.)

NINA. Sooo . . . Chicago is your home turf. Gonna do "I Don't Wanna Grow Up" again tonight?

SHREDDY. Indeed. Johnny Ramone and I are in this together.

(NINA gives him a look.)

SHREDDY. What??

NINA. I mean, so many Ramones songs objectively rock harder.

SHREDDY. Were that true, WERE that true, and I'm not saying it is, how hard a song rocks or how technically impressive it is, is NOT the only thing to consider when choosing a song. Everything about "I Don't Wanna Grow Up" makes it perfect for air guitar, for me, and for the Central Conference Finals.

NINA. *(exaggerated)* Gooo ooon.

SHREDDY. The Ramones are from Forest Hills, Queens. I am from the South Side of Chicago. We are in Chicago now. This is all urban kismet.

NINA. "I Wanna Be Sedated" is better-known.

CANNIBAL QUEEN. Then why are you here trying to intimidate her?

VICIOUS. I'm a guest of the organizers. They asked me to pick the Round Two song.

CANNIBAL QUEEN. You could've done that over email.

VICIOUS. I'm here in person to support my friends.

CANNIBAL QUEEN. Bullshit. You haven't given a crap about any of these people, including me, since your Sprite commercial hit YouTube. *(softer)* You used to be the most fun guy on the whole circuit, Vicious. The absolute most fun guy to be around backstage, or in the green room, or at the hotel. It didn't matter how you did onstage on a particular night, you were always excited to be in the room. That's the guy I want to be around. That's the guy we all want to be around. And I don't know if he even exists anymore.

VICIOUS. *(a moment of real vulnerability)* It's real easy to be the "fun guy" when you don't have anything to lose. You guys have nowhere to go but up. There's a huge target on my back, and all of you act like it's not there. Like nothing's different now. Everything is different now. *(resuming his persona)* I have a legacy to protect.

CANNIBAL QUEEN. *(not letting him off the hook)* Well if your "legacy" is all you care about anymore, then you *should* be scared of The Nina. You've got the charisma on lock, Vicious, but she's a better guitarist than you. I've seen it. I watched your old band videos online.

VICIOUS. You did what?

CANNIBAL QUEEN. Come on, they're on YouTube. It's not like I hacked your computer.

VICIOUS. That's still fucking weird.

CANNIBAL QUEEN. She hasn't played since Staten Island, how else am I supposed to know what I'm up against? I'll say this: I've never seen two people in the same band who more wanted to be solo acts.

VICIOUS. Real nice.

CANNIBAL QUEEN. The Nina's got terrible stage presence, and she's totally in her head, but she's got good musicality. I've seen that girl literally everywhere this season—she knows everyone's strategies. If she shows up here tonight and pounds it out enough to qualify, she's gonna come at us hard in the championship.

VICIOUS. Nina's a decent guitarist. I don't know that she's better than me, I don't know why you would say that, except to piss me off, but she's decent. But this is all a vendetta thing for her. She doesn't have the heart. And she's never gonna win Nationals. For fuckssake, she's a . . . *(he stops himself)*

CANNIBAL QUEEN. Yes?

VICIOUS. *(covering)* Nothing.

CANNIBAL QUEEN. She's a girl? She'll never sweep Nationals because she's a girl?

VICIOUS. You're putting words in my mouth.

CANNIBAL QUEEN. Then deny that's what you thought.

VICIOUS. FINE. I thought it. But I didn't say it.

CANNIBAL QUEEN. That's bad enough. *(pause, a realization)* You never, for a single moment, thought that I had any chance at beating you. Did you?

VICIOUS. *(losing it)* You don't!

CANNIBAL QUEEN. Prick!

VICIOUS. You don't! What, like that's big news? I shred harder, I work the crowd better . . . you . . . You give the audience something to look at between real competitors.

CANNIBAL QUEEN. Fuck off and die!

VICIOUS. I have to be twice as good as you, because I don't get to flash my panties and bat my eyelashes. Instead of whining and crying about how girls never win, I don't know, Astrid, why don't you *fucking work harder*, huh? You have every advantage that I do, plus more, so don't point your finger at me and say I'm keeping you down. You have no idea what it's like, as a dude, to work and sweat and rehearse for weeks, cut together the perfect song, drive for hours to compete, and then get upstaged by a pair of tits that just showed up to have fun.

CANNIBAL QUEEN. Is that honestly what you think I am? You think I don't take this as seriously as you do?

VICIOUS. You don't have to when you start on third base. But you know what? You can't touch me. I'm channeling the rage and glory of my forefathers. That's why I'm not scared of you, OR Nina. You're a sideshow around here. I'm the main event.

CANNIBAL QUEEN. I see you. Holy shit, I see you for real, David Cooper. And you're a moron.

(They are both furious. A beat of silence.

The door to the bar opens, and NINA *is standing there.* NINA *is dressed, for the first time, like an air guitar goddess. She sees the two of them, feels the tension in the air, but before she can speak,* CANNIBAL QUEEN *grabs her hand and drags her into the green room. Lights dim on the bar, and* VICIOUS.

Lights up on the green room. GOLDEN, FACEBENDER, *and* SHREDDY *are sitting on the couches. They look toward the door as* CANNIBAL QUEEN *blows in like a hurricane, dragging* NINA *behind her.)*

GOLDEN. Hey! Wha—what is happening?

CANNIBAL QUEEN. *(to* NINA, *ignoring everyone else)* What song are you doing tonight?

NINA. I—I don't—

CANNIBAL QUEEN. Vicious is here to knock you off your game. I hope you found a killer song, and you're prepared to throw down, because the biggest mindfuck you can give that dickbag is to absolutely slay tonight. *(Pause, she evaluates* NINA's *outfit for the first time)* Congrats on not dressing like a prostitute. At least that point got through.

FACEBENDER. What a fierce and beautiful partnership!

GOLDEN. Hold on. CQ, did you and Vicious break up?

CANNIBAL QUEEN. *(icily)* I have ended our arrangement.

(Unseen by CANNIBAL QUEEN, FACEBENDER *straightens his wig and takes a hopeful step toward her.)*

CANNIBAL QUEEN. That is in no way any kind of invitation to anyone in this room.

*(*FACEBENDER *is crestfallen. He takes a step back.* CANNIBAL QUEEN *notices nothing.)*

SHREDDY. What song ARE you doing for freestyle tonight, The Nina?

NINA. Guys, I— I really— I don't know if I can do this.

SHREDDY. *(simultaneously)* What?!

CANNIBAL QUEEN. *(simultaneously)* Oh fuck, he got to you.

NINA. I have pages and pages of notes and I've watched every video, and I've rehearsed for hours, but I'm terrified I'm going to get up there and shut down again.

CANNIBAL QUEEN. Like you did at the Hungry Brain two years ago?

NINA. How do you—? You watched our band videos?

CANNIBAL QUEEN. They are *on the internet*. Why is everyone so shocked?

NINA. But why—

CANNIBAL QUEEN. *(interrupting)* Do you know what your problem is?

NINA. *(frustrated)* I'm sure *you* do.

CANNIBAL QUEEN. You can't stop looking at yourself.

(NINA *says nothing.*)

CANNIBAL QUEEN. Air guitar, "there" guitar, it's the same thing. I know that look. You're not inside the music, you're not onstage, you're in the audience, judging yourself. That's something that rehearsal is not gonna to fix. You gotta get up onstage and work through that shit.

(NINA *says nothing. This is an old issue for her, and* CANNIBAL QUEEN *has hit the nail on the head.*)

CANNIBAL QUEEN. You wanna know why I show up in these shitty bars month after month and *pretend* to do a thing I can *actually* do better than just about anyone in the world?

FACEBENDER. Yes.

CANNIBAL QUEEN. Because there is a shield that I have to carry, all around myself, all day, every day, just to be safe and move through the world. All the parts of myself that are freaky or loud or ugly or dangerous have to stay tucked inside, so I don't feel what dudes shout at me on the street, or say about me in the goddamn halls of Congress. But when I get onstage, sister, I can put that shield down and let all my darkness come rushing out.

NINA. Wow.

CANNIBAL QUEEN. When's the last time you felt that free, The Nina?

NINA. Um. Before puberty?

CANNIBAL QUEEN. Let it go, girl. Just take a breath, tell that voice in your head to go fuck itself, and raise hell.

NINA. But why would anyone want to see me up there, when they could see you?

GOLDEN. Air guitar is not about "or." It's about "and."

FACEBENDER. Another glorious truism.

GOLDEN. *(shrugging)* It's a gift.

SHREDDY. He's right, The Nina. It's not about whether the world *needs* another badass air guitarist. It's about how *you feel* when you're up there. It's the pure joy of jumping around naked in your bedroom, but in front of screaming fans.

GOLDEN. So get your head outta your notes and your ass up onstage. Otherwise, what has all of this been for, The Nina?

NINA. *(pause, she decides)* You're right. I have to do this. It's been months since Staten Island. I'm basically a new person now.

CANNIBAL QUEEN. And what is this new person's song?

NINA. *(smirking)* "Crowd Chant."

   (The entire group falls silent.)

NINA. What? What?! It kills! *(she turns to SHREDDY)* Shreddy, you know that track kills.

   (SHREDDY just shrugs at her. CANNIBAL QUEEN shakes her head.)

CANNIBAL QUEEN. Oh, girl.

NINA. What?!

FACEBENDER. *(delicately)* Miss The Nina, is it possible that you are only playing this song as a way to thumb your nose at one particular person in the crowd?

NINA. What? No. What does that even mean?

CANNIBAL QUEEN. It's a huge fuck you to Vicious. You know that song almost got him fired from his Sprite commercial. Just admit it.

NINA. Joe Satriani!

GOLDEN. Denial!

NINA. Why are you so upset?

GOLDEN. Because you are trying to take air guitar and weaponize it! It's basically sacrilegious.

CANNIBAL QUEEN. Also, bad strategy. Vicious gets to pick the Round Two song tonight. And he can change it at any time.

NINA. So?

CANNIBAL QUEEN. So do you really want to provoke him?

NINA. I don't care what Vicious thinks.

GOLDEN. Uh, clearly you do.

NINA. "Crowd Chant." Joe Satriani. It's gonna slay. I'm gonna win. End of discussion.

(NINA *exits, excited and smug.*)

SHREDDY. How, after all these months, does she still not get it?

NINA'S SECOND PERFORMANCE

(*Lights shift quickly.* NINA *takes the stage in New York.*)

[#11: *"Crowd Chant" clip*]

(*We see* NINA *play the last line of her cut of the song from D Vicious's Sprite Commercial. She seems very pleased, and the crowd is cheering loudly. We know she's done pretty well in the first round.* VICIOUS *scowls at her.*)

ANNOUNCER. All right! Let's hear it for The Nina! Okay, folks, we are moving into to Round Two here in New York!

(VICIOUS *walks out onstage in front of the other competitors. The crowd goes nuts. He whispers in the* ANNOUCER's *ear.*)

ANNOUNCER. Your champ, D Vicious, has selected our compulsory track tonight, and actually just pulled a little switcheroo on us just now, but I gotta say, the choice is pretty epic. Hit it!

[#12: *"You Give Love a Bad Name"*]

(*We hear a cut of a real "piss off" breakup rock song: Bon Jovi's "You Give Love a Bad Name".*
This is 100% directed at NINA — *it's the song he left playing when he bailed on her [as referenced in Scene 3].*

VICIOUS *smirks as the song plays, taunting* NINA. *After a moment, the song fades down so we can hear the following dialogue.*)

NINA. (*stunned*) Oh. Very mature.

CANNIBAL QUEEN. Holy shit, son.

GOLDEN. The clapback on this just reached epic level.

FACEBENDER. Ruthless.

GOLDEN. Genius.

SHREDDY. Heartless.

NINA. Hopeless.

(*The cut of the breakup song fades back up and* NINA *begins to play. She's okay at it, not the best, and definitely thrown off.*

She finishes the round on an okay note. We hear some applause. But it won't be good enough.)

Scene 6: New York—After the Loss / Invite to the Dark Horse

(Lights up on the green room of the previous scene's bar in New York. It is an hour or so after the Eastern Conference Finals. NINA is sadly packing up her stuff or changing into street clothes. It's over for her, and she doesn't want to stick around.)

SHREDDY. *(reassuring)* It was your first year. And you showed up in a big way. You weren't bad out there tonight, you just . . .

NINA. Weren't good enough?

SHREDDY. Well, yeah. *(short pause)* No. No, you know what, screw that, you slayed. You had the technique, your choreography was killer, everyone could see—

NINA. *(interrupting)* My heart was in the wrong place and my song was a dick move.

SHREDDY. None of us could have predicted Vicious would go nuclear in Round Two.

NINA. But I should have been ready, no matter what the song. That's what you trained me for. I thought I HAD it. But you knew I didn't. Y'all tried to tell me. I'm such a fucking idiot.

(SHREDDY makes a decision. He takes out his phone and finds something. He hands it to NINA.)

SHREDDY. I want to show you something.

NINA. *(wearily)* What?

SHREDDY. *(referring to the video on his phone)* This is my first-ever competition. Chicago, four years ago. I warn you, it's pretty brutal.

NINA. It can't be worse than my first qualifier.

[#13: "Sweet Child of Mine" phone clip]

(NINA hits "play." We hear the opening chords of "Sweet Child of Mine" coming from the phone. They watch for a moment.)

NINA. *(incredulous)* What?! You—!

SHREDDY. *(interrupting)* It was their best-charting song in the US!

NINA. *(watching a bit more of the video)* This performance is pretty upsetting. *(short pause)* WHOA!

SHREDDY. YEAH. Some douche-canoe took off his shoe and chucked it at me.

NINA. I see that.

SHREDDY. And I completely sucked.

NINA. *(analytical, not meaning to be complimentary or flirty)* I mean, I guess. But enthusiasm counts for a lot. You've clearly always had that in spades.

SHREDDY. You're just being nice.

NINA. *(still not meaning to flirt)* I'm being honest. There's something about you onstage that's magnetic. Even when you're totally bombing.

SHREDDY. *(blushing a little)* I didn't even make it to the second round that night. So why would a guy who shit the bed that hard his first time out, ever EVER, want to play air guitar again?

NINA. Because it's not about "me," it's about "we." Golden Thunder told me that.

SHREDDY. Exactly. I went back to the green room that first night, in absolute shame, trying to sneak out the back door. But before I could make my escape, Golden was there. And Cannibal Queen. Facebender. Satan's Sidekick. Mazel Tov Cocktail. Captain Air-Merica. They bought me shots. We laughed together. They didn't mock me. They didn't kick me out because I'd failed. We all fail. That's part of it. And we're all still here.

NINA. You found your people that night.

SHREDDY. Exactly. And I think we're your people, too. But we're pretty pushy about collaboration.

NINA. I've noticed. And I think I might be ready to hang up the lone wolf act.

SHREDDY. Very cool.

NINA. *(a little hesitant)* And . . . even though the season's almost over . . . If I wanted to keep spending time with you. Just one-on-one? Would you be into that? Maybe we could check out some music or—

SHREDDY. *(eagerly interrupting)* Yeah— I'd—I'd be really into that. Yes.

(They both smile. NINA looks back at SHREDDY's phone.)

NINA. You dodged that shoe like a ninja.

SHREDDY. You're going to watch it again?

NINA. Not right now. Later, for sure. Like, a buuuuunch of times.

(SHREDDY snatches his phone from NINA. She grins at him. He grins back.

Suddenly, without warning, a HOODED FIGURE [by which I mean he is wearing a hoodie and the hood is up] enters, carrying a large black envelope. There is ominous, gothic music coming from his pocket [playing on his phone or a small Bluetooth speaker].

The HOODED FIGURE *proceeds directly to* NINA *and hands her the envelope.* GOLDEN, CANNIBAL QUEEN, *and* FACEBENDER *are silently following him into the room, eyes wide.)*

HOODED FIGURE. Prepare yourself, The Nina. The Dark Horse competition begins in two hours.

(The HOODED FIGURE *exits.* NINA *is confused. Everyone else is stunned.)*

GOLDEN. Holy mother of god, is that what I think it is?

CANNIBAL QUEEN. I . . . I've never seen one in real life.

FACEBENDER. We saw the Hooded Figure moving through the arena and were compelled to follow. But who could have foreseen that his destination was The Nina?

NINA. Um, what am I holding?

GOLDEN. The Nina. That is a motherfucking invitation to the motherfucking Dark Horse Round.

NINA. I need more information.

FACEBENDER. That is your ticket to glory, M'lady.

SHREDDY. When all the qualifiers are over, the Air Guitar organizers hold a Dark Horse competition. It's one round, sudden death, invitation-only. And the winner gets to go to Nationals.

NINA. Really?! Why am I only hearing about this now?

SHREDDY. *(this is obvious)* You can't plan on a Dark Horse! We never know when it will be, or where, or who the organizers will invite.

CANNIBAL QUEEN. They're giving you another shot. They see potential in you.

NINA. Potential for what?

ALL except NINA. *(in unison)* Airness.

CANNIBAL QUEEN. And if you expect to win, that's what you're gonna have to give them.

NINA. Great. To go to Nationals, I have to give the judges a thing that none of you can even explain to me.

SHREDDY. *(parsing it out)* Airness is like . . . like, okay, we're here, we're like, miming, some of the greatest guitar licks ever played, right? We're paying homage to those songs, those guitarists. It's like what little kids do, they hear this music, it gets inside them, and then they have to flip out about it. That's where air guitar comes from, from a time before you cared about looking cool. You're just trying to get inside the thing.

GOLDEN. Airness is when you actually do get inside the thing.

(NINA *sighs in exasperation.*)

SHREDDY. It's like . . . great stage magic.

CANNIBAL QUEEN. Or drag.

SHREDDY. Yeah! You're not paying homage anymore. You're the creator of something totally new.

FACEBENDER. You've . . . transcended.

NINA. Transcended not having an actual guitar in my hands?

CANNIBAL QUEEN. Exactly.

SHREDDY. You're expressing something as true and as free and as powerful as Hendrix or Prince or Malmsteen or Joan Jett, but you're doing it without an instrument.

CANNIBAL QUEEN. Did you throw Joan Jett in there because she's a girl?

SHREDDY. Joan Jett started the Runaways when she was 17 and she is *still* touring. She has *never* taken a year off. Her first solo album was rejected by 23 record labels and she kept right on going. There is no one on the face of God's green earth more rockstar than Joan Jett. Fight me.

NINA. THANK you.

GOLDEN. Airness isn't unattainable. It's just that hardly anyone ever gets there.

(*They all silently contemplate the ineffable essence of airness.*)

CANNIBAL QUEEN. You've got airness inside you, waiting to get out. But first, we gotta know: WHAT'S. YOUR. SONG? You need a completely new tactic for the Dark Horse.

NINA. How am I supposed to pick the perfect song under this kind of pressure?!

SHREDDY. Hive mind—activate!

(SHREDDY *spins around to each of them, in turn. They build on each other's suggestions, interrupting each other and finishing other's thoughts, creating a swirling atmosphere of collaboration.*)

SHREDDY. Golden Thunder! What should our girl play and why?

GOLDEN. Um . . . "Cherry Bomb." In male drag.

SHREDDY. Okay, great stuff, but—

CANNIBAL QUEEN. *(interrupting)* Ha!

GOLDEN. It's a slam-dunk! It's—

CANNIBAL QUEEN. *(interrupting)* The Runaways are a punk band, that's a punk song, it's vocal-driven. Think bigger!

SHREDDY. What's your suggestion?

CANNIBAL QUEEN. Nina. I think you could handle Steve—

CANNIBAL QUEEN/FACEBENDER. *(in unison)* —Vai!

FACEBENDER. Steven Vai! Capital!

CANNIBAL QUEEN. "For the Love of God" is a technical masterpiece!

SHREDDY. But that's what *you* do, Cannibal Queen.

GOLDEN. Yeah, you can't both be the one with flawless technique.

CANNIBAL QUEEN. *(she knows he's right)* Shit.

SHREDDY. *(to FACEBENDER)* You are our only hope! Save us, aged one!

FACEBENDER. *(dropping his façade)* Dude, what have I told you about the age jokes?

SHREDDY. *(sincerely)* Sorry.

FACEBENDER. *(resuming his façade)* Nevertheless, I am prepared to come to your rescue, fair The Nina. I submit "I Believe in a Thing Called Love."

GOLDEN. *(simultaneously)* Great song! And it has AMAZING costume opportunities.

CANNIBAL QUEEN. *(simultaneously)* Crowdbait. It's showmanship and mushy shtick. It's—

FACEBENDER. *(interrupting, in earnest)* It is an ode to romantic yearning! Have you never had your hopes set on someone who stretched your heart beyond its limits?

> *(A short pause. Will CANNIBAL QUEEN finally realize that she is his Dulcinea?)*

CANNIBAL QUEEN. If you've totally forfeited your taste, why not just play some Sammy Hagar Van Halen and be done with it?

> *(FACEBENDER, SHREDDY, and GOLDEN groan, like, "how DARE you?" FACEBENDER is hit especially hard.)*

NINA. *(over their groans)* That song just doesn't feel like my . . . guts.

FACEBENDER. *(sighing)* Fair enough.

CANNIBAL QUEEN. I assume you have a suggestion, Shreddy?

SHREDDY. Of course I do. And it's a hands-down winner. *(short dramatic pause)* "Everlong." Foo Fighters.

FACEBENDER. *(simultaneously)* Alas!

GOLDEN. *(simultaneously)* Satan's Sidekick already qualified with "Everlong."

SHREDDY. Motörhead? Hendrix? Vaughn?

GOLDEN. *(simultaneously)* Taken, taken, taken.

FACEBENDER. *(simultaneously)* Alas, alas, alas.

(NINA has been thinking hard, getting inspired.)

GOLDEN. Okay, how does everyone feel about Swedish Death Metal, it's a—

NINA. *(interrupting)* Wait, wait, everybody shut up. Shreddy, what was that thing you said about airness? . . . That . . . air guitar comes from a time before you cared about looking cool?

SHREDDY. Yeah. Like when you were a kid, and you'd just flip out.

NINA. Right. That's where my song lives! In my kidhood, jumping around at slumber parties, knocking the other girls over because I couldn't control my arms. It's maybe not cool, or difficult, or flashy, but it's in my bones. That's where I'm gonna find my airness.

SHREDDY. What's that song, The Nina? Do you have it?

NINA. *(pause, discovering)* Yeah. Yeah, I have it.

CANNIBAL QUEEN. Fantastic. We have two hours until the Dark Horse.

(GOLDEN holds up a glue gun and a fistful of sequins or feathers that he has conjured from seemingly nowhere.)

GOLDEN. Let's get to work.

(Lights dim on the green room.)

Vignette 3: The Dark Horse Competition

(There is a scenic transition into a very different world than any we've been in. It feels like we've landed in a dark air guitar skulls/

fight club world that reminds us a little of the "Total Eclipse of the Heart" music video.

NINA enters and a box of light appears in the center of the stage. She walks into it.)

ANNOUNCER. *(booming voice, very ominous reverb, seems to be coming from everywhere)* Gentlemen of the Jury, your next Dark Horse competitor—THE NINA.

NINA'S DARK HORSE PERFORMANCE

[#14: "Shadows of the Night"]

(The music begins, and NINA loses her mind to Pat Benatar's "Shadows of the Night."

In competitive air guitar, the performer may be aided by other performers as long as they are not onstage. SHREDDY, CANNIBAL QUEEN, FACEBENDER, *and* GOLDEN *all participate—they throw confetti, they wave streamers, they hold up floor fans to blow Nina's hair and costume around. This number is a triumph of collaboration. THIS MUST BE A GROUP NUMBER.*

NINA is overflowing with joy. She is exuberant, she is fun embodied. Not self-conscious, not mocking, not afraid of anything. The judges see all this.)

ANNOUNCER. *(booming voice, very ominous reverb, seems to be coming from everywhere)* Gentlemen, I believe we have our Dark Horse champion. We will see you at the National Championship, The Nina.

(NINA's friends crowd around her, ecstatic.
Lights dim on the Dark Horse competition.)

Scene 7: Los Angeles—The National Championship

(Lights up on an extremely large, very glam stage in Los Angeles. It's a cavernous, glitzy bar where famous bands have played for decades, or a big outdoor arena like the Greek.

VICIOUS is onstage, giving an interview to the ANNOUNCER, who is an air guitar organizer in this scene. They speak into microphones.

There might be roadies and other people milling around, setting up for the concert. There might even be a video camera set up, recording the interview.)

ANNOUNCER. Okay, okay, okay, LA. I'm here with our reigning National Air Guitar champ, D Vicious, to talk shop about tonight's National Finals competition. How are you feeling today, Champ?

VICIOUS. Ready to slay. I want another shot at Oulu.

ANNOUNCER. Wow, already focused on the World Finals, huh? Aren't you worried about tonight?

VICIOUS. No. I'm not worried.

ANNOUNCER. Bold words, bold words!

VICIOUS. My greatest competition has always been, and will always be, myself. And right now, we're pretty in sync with each other.

ANNOUNCER. Spoken like a true villain, Vicious! All right, I'll take the bait, let's talk about you. What was your championship year like? You win Nationals, there's so much buzz, but then it's the off-season. What's February like for D Vicious?

VICIOUS. *(at a loss)* I mean, it's Black History Month.

ANNOUNCER. Okay, true, true, but like, what have you been *working on?* Can you give us a hint about what you're gonna throw down tonight?

VICIOUS. Let me ask you a better question—why mess with success?

ANNOUNCER. Uh—

VICIOUS. *(interrupting)* If it works, work it, man.

ANNOUNCER. *(refocusing the interview)* One last question before we go. It's been said by some of the greats that air guitar is the only true abstract art form left, because it can't be commercialized. You faced some backlash from fans last year, when you starred in an online commercial for a soft drink. Care to comment?

VICIOUS. *(annoyed)* Well, I mean, if those fans who are upset about my "corruption" of their "pure" "art form" want to send me checks to cover my bills, they're more than welcome to. You can only do something for the love of it up to a certain level, you know? After a while, the things you've paid into need to start paying you back.

(The ANNOUNCER realizes he better wrap this up real quick.)

ANNOUNCER. Well that's just about all the time we have for today. Come out and see D Vicious and the rest of our bitchin' finalists at the Air Guitar National Championships, happening tonight!

VICIOUS. Come out and watch us slay tonight, LA. I promise to melt your faces.

(The ANNOUNCER shakes VICIOUS's hand and exits. VICIOUS exits.

NINA and SHREDDY are revealed on the side of the stage. They've been watching this whole thing.)

NINA. Hey, have you ever watched the outtakes of his Sprite commercial? Almost makes you feel sorry for him.

SHREDDY. Yeah. Almost. *(envious)* He's gonna have the most advantageous spot in the lineup tonight.

NINA. But we have something he's lost.

SHREDDY. Raw fucking joy?

NINA. Raw fucking joy.

(They beam at each other.

GOLDEN, FACEBENDER, and CANNIBAL QUEEN join them onstage, hugging and high-fiving. They are all totally amped.

(LIGHTS COME UP IN A BIG WAY!! Sound cue!! Fog?! Suddenly, they're actual rock stars. We hear a screaming crowd, dimly, in the distance. It's MOTHERFUCKING EPIC. The audience is like, "Holy shit. This is for real." Electricity in the air!)

NINA. This is amazing!!

SHREDDY. It truly is. Every time.

NINA. *(looking at him with wonder)* This is where you've been the whole time. In your mind. Even back in Staten Island, you were here. You've always been here.

(His face lights up, he stares at her, she stares at him. Amped.)

VICIOUS'S PERFORMANCE

(VICIOUS takes center stage.)

ANNOUNCER. And here he is, folks! Our reigning American Air Guitar Champ, back to defend his title, his honor, NAY his glory! Put your filthy hands together for: D! VICIOUS!

> [#15: "*Cum on Feel the Noize*" *slo-mo clip*]
>
> (VICIOUS *raises his hands over his head. We hear the crowd cheer. He brings his hands in front of him and begins to play, and we hear the first few notes of "Cum on Feel the Noize"—THE SAME SONG HE PLAYED IN THE PROLOGUE! But then the track slows down into a weird, slo-mo warped version. VICIOUS looks ridiculous. Exactly as ridiculous as a man playing slo-mo air guitar to a distorted track. It's a rote performance, crafted and rehearsed, but devoid of heart.*
>
> *The music fades down, but not out. The others watch* VICIOUS, *and comment during his bizarre song.*)

NINA. Incredible.

GOLDEN. He fuckin' *hates* this.

SHREDDY. More than hates it. It's a joke to him. He's gotten so good that he's actually come *back around* to mockery.

GOLDEN. Mockery is the enemy of airness.

NINA. *(to* GOLDEN*)* And If you pick the wrong song, rehearsal is kind of irrelevant.

GOLDEN. Exactly.

FACEBENDER. He resembles a tortured animal, forced to perform for loathéd masses.

CANNIBAL QUEEN. This is some sad, sad shit.

SHREDDY. Who does the same song two years in a row? That's not just unwise—it's fucking unFUN.

NINA. *(determined and excited)* People. The old guard has fallen. Let's storm this motherfuckin' castle.

> (GOLDEN *puts his hand out, like they're going to circle up in a sports movie.*)

GOLDEN. "Airness" on three! *(pause)* "Airness" on three, guys!

CANNIBAL QUEEN. Nope. We're not doing that.

GOLDEN. *(unfazed)* Okay. But know I'm doing it. *(he taps his heart)* In here.

(VICIOUS finishes his slo-mo song.

Lights shift quickly. GOLDEN, SHREDDY, FACEBENDER, NINA, *and* CANNIBAL QUEEN *line up across the bar's stage, joining* VICIOUS. NINA *in the middle. We hear a sound cue of a HUGE, enthusiastic, cheering crowd. Thousands of people. Drunk, happy, losing their damn minds.*

As the ANNOUNCER *says their names, each character steps forward and strikes his/her superhero pose.)*

ANNOUNCER. Okay, people, here we are at ROUND TWO! You know what comes next for our National Championship finalists!
From the East Coast: GOLDEN THUNDER!
Repping the Western Conference: FACEBENDER!
Your Mid-Atlantic champ: CANNIBAL QUEEN!
Central Conference Victor: SHREDDY EDDY!
Your Dark Horse Heroine: THE NINA!
And reigning champion D VICIOUS!
And now, without any ado, here is the song the judges have selected for Round Two of tonight's National Championship.

[#16: "I Love Rock 'N Roll"]

(The competitors stand very still to catch the first strains of the music. A beat of silence; even the crowd's cheering falls away. WHAT SONG WILL IT BE? We hear the first few notes of Joan Jett and Blackhearts's "I Love Rock and Roll." NINA *punches the air.)*

NINA. Joan! Fucking! JETT!!

(The finalists begin playing, one by one, down the line. [In reality, they would be taking turns, but for our purposes, we will just stagger their starts]. Everyone is rocking hard, except VICIOUS; *his heart is obviously not in this.*

Last of all, NINA *plays. She's been longing to play Joan Jett all along. She's inside the music. She's a child, she's a woman, she's having the time of her life. She's also, still, a fantastic guitarist. She's not paying homage, she's not pretending to do anything, she has transcended. SHE'S FOUND THE AIRNESS. The others stop playing, one by one, and watch her in awe. Even* VICIOUS *can't compete, and just stares at her.*

NINA *finishes playing the song cut just as the* ANNOUNCER *enters. An instrumental version of the song plays through the end of the scene.)*

[#17: "I Love Rock 'N Roll" instrumental]

ANNOUNCER. It was a close one here tonight, folks, but the judges have made their decision. This year's Air Guitar National Champion, who'll be repping Uncle Sam at the World Championships in Finland, is: THE NINA!!

(VICIOUS stomps offstage. The others crowd around NINA, sharing in her glory.)

SHREDDY. *(very excited for her)* Fuck you! I demand a recount!

NINA. *(grabbing him)* Come here.

(NINA grabs SHREDDY and kisses him.)

GOLDEN. That was some true airness, people. I'm just glad I got to see it in my lifetime.

CANNIBAL QUEEN. Me too, Golden. Me too.

(GOLDEN turns and sees the kissing.)

GOLDEN. Aw, look at this!

FACEBENDER. *(earnestly)* I just love love stories. Don't you?

(CANNIBAL QUEEN turns to FACEBENDER, as though she's really seeing him for the first time.)

CANNIBAL QUEEN. *(sincerely)* Yeah. I really fucking do.

(The music swells. Blackout.)

End of Play